CAMBRIDGE I

Books of

MW00830562

Literary Studies

This series provides a high-quality selection of early printings of literary works, textual editions, anthologies and literary criticism which are of lasting scholarly interest. Ranging from Old English to Shakespeare to early twentieth-century work from around the world, these books offer a valuable resource for scholars in reception history, textual editing, and literary studies.

The Principles of the Art of Conversation

The classical scholar J.P. Mahaffy (1839–1919) is known equally for his work on Greek texts and Egyptian papyri (several of his books are reissued in the Cambridge Library Collection). He graduated from Trinity College, Dublin, and spent the rest of his working life there, as a fellow, and ultimately as provost from 1914 until his death. This light-hearted book was published in 1887, and the 1888 second edition, with Mahaffy's responses to his critics in the preface, is reissued here. His approach is to analyse the art of conversation in the same way that a classical scholar would analyse the art of rhetoric, discussing theoretical models as well as taking examples from history and from his own social life. However, after considering all aspects of conversation, including its universality and necessity, Mahaffy concludes that 'the perfect practice of it is a mystery, which defies analysis'.

Cambridge University Press has long been a pioneer in the reissuing of out-of-print titles from its own backlist, producing digital reprints of books that are still sought after by scholars and students but could not be reprinted economically using traditional technology. The Cambridge Library Collection extends this activity to a wider range of books which are still of importance to researchers and professionals, either for the source material they contain, or as landmarks in the history of their academic discipline.

Drawing from the world-renowned collections in the Cambridge University Library and other partner libraries, and guided by the advice of experts in each subject area, Cambridge University Press is using state-of-the-art scanning machines in its own Printing House to capture the content of each book selected for inclusion. The files are processed to give a consistently clear, crisp image, and the books finished to the high quality standard for which the Press is recognised around the world. The latest print-on-demand technology ensures that the books will remain available indefinitely, and that orders for single or multiple copies can quickly be supplied.

The Cambridge Library Collection brings back to life books of enduring scholarly value (including out-of-copyright works originally issued by other publishers) across a wide range of disciplines in the humanities and social sciences and in science and technology.

The Principles of the Art of Conversation
A Social Essay

John Pentland Mahaffy

CAMBRIDGE
UNIVERSITY PRESS

CAMBRIDGE
UNIVERSITY PRESS

University Printing House, Cambridge, CB2 8BS, United Kingdom

Cambridge University Press is part of the University of Cambridge.

It furthers the University's mission by disseminating knowledge in the pursuit of education, learning and research at the highest international levels of excellence.

www.cambridge.org
Information on this title: www.cambridge.org/9781108078634

This edition first published 1888
This digitally printed version 2017

ISBN 978-1-108-07863-4 Paperback

THE PRINCIPLES

OF THE

ART OF CONVERSATION

THE PRINCIPLES

OF THE

ART OF CONVERSATION

A SOCIAL ESSAY

BY

J. P. MAHAFFY

SECOND EDITION

REVISED AND ENLARGED

London

MACMILLAN AND CO.

AND NEW YORK

1888

First Edition, 1887
Second Edition, 1888

TO

MY SILENT FRIENDS

PREFACE

THE prompt appearance of this new edition gives me an opportunity of thanking the many critics who reviewed the book for both their suggestions and their strictures, as well as of making some observations upon the latter where they seem to me reasonable. Frequently, indeed, I was reminded of what I had not forgotten, and presented with what I not only knew but had plainly set down in the following pages, which my censors had not taken the trouble to read. It is amusing to add that two persons, who utterly despised the book, and publicly declared it to be worthless, were themselves once thought agreeable, and admitted to good society, but have long since been dropped, because their conversation had become intolerably tedious or objectionable. My fair readers who are not versed in logic may take this as an argument in favour of my work. To me it only implies that the book is serious, and therefore disappointing to that class of talker who expected to find in it a new *Joe Miller*, with anecdotes to last for a few nights, and pass for original till their source was detected. To compile a book of this kind is a degrading task, from which most authors would turn with aversion.

This objection, then, was really an ob-

jection to the seriousness and dryness of
a theory set forth in strict form.

It is balanced by a widely contrasted line
of criticism, which asserted that the work
was exceedingly frivolous, and painfully
worldly. The good people who felt this
were probably moved by my strictures on
over-solemnity in conversation, still more
by the deliberate theory underlying my
whole argument, that *recreation, and not
improvement, is the proper object of conversation.* All kinds of intellectual and moral
knowledge are, no doubt, conveyed by
talking as their natural vehicle. Much of
the highest education is obtained through
it. There is no object of human life,
however serious, which does not depend
upon the exposition and discussion of
men. But in all these higher cases con-

versation is only a means. When it becomes an end, it is prosecuted for recreation's sake, that is to say, for its own
sake, and this is the point of view from
which a theorist must approach it. Then
all the higher interests of life become in
their turn means, and means for the
purpose of recreation. No serious theory
of conversation is therefore possible which
does not regard it as an end, and the
subordination of higher things to this end
is no proof of frivolity, but rather of the
very reverse.

It seems very hard indeed to steer without cavil between the censors of seriousness
and the censors of frivolity. It was objected
that I spoke with disrespect of the weather,
and again with respect of politics, as
topics of conversation. The latter I even

recommended as a study for ladies who desire to be agreeable. Many grave and wise people told me that ladies have no business with politics, and that talking upon such subjects with them is highly objectionable. They told me they greatly preferred the company of a woman who knew no politics. On the other hand, the highest female authority within my knowledge—the authoress of the excellent book on *Moral Teaching*, who has spent a long life in trying to improve women socially as well as morally—has been good enough to send me word that she is on my side.

Further reflection confirms me in the opinion that I was right, and that if the good people who are afraid of female politicians had gone more into the world, and made themselves acquainted with other

societies than their own, they would have
discovered that women who know no politics
cannot rank in the first class, and that this
want is one of the commonest marks of
provincial, as compared with metropolitan,
society. There are many men who have
never met any but commonplace women,
and who hardly know what a brilliant
woman is like. They imagine that no
woman can understand and talk of politics
without being a strong-minded female who
will tolerate nothing else, and will attempt
to put down opposing men. Instead of
this imaginary bugbear of the middle
classes, it would be easy to show them
real examples of ladies whose traditions
are political, whose relatives are politicians, whose reading is mostly politics, and
who therefore exceed in smartness and

general intelligence of conversation not only the ordinary piano-playing young woman, and the ordinary *Hausfrau*, but all the more frivolous members of their own class. I refuse, therefore, to abandon my position, for I have found the woman who understands politics to be superior, *from my special point of view*, to her homelier sister. And as I said in my earlier Preface, all the types in this book are drawn from real life.

It will amuse the reader to know that among those who thought themselves the models of these types,[1] the great majority wished to be identified as the *sympathetic listener* (p. 69), thus indicating that after all they held talking, however good, to be

---

[1] It was surprising how many found in their own portraits an exact likeness of somebody else.

a doubtful virtue, perhaps little better than an amiable weakness. Nor is this surprising, seeing that so many great talkers are bad talkers, tedious, pertinacious, noisy, quarrelsome. If so, this feeling more than justifies any attempt to improve conversation not only by practice, but by discussing its theory.

There is one piece of negative evidence that this latter, as I conceived it, is complete. No omission of any importance has been pointed out to me, though I have sought everywhere for suggestions to make this edition more worthy of the public favour.

One point, which might fairly be added to § 35, was given to me after the sheets had gone through the press, and I gladly add it here.

In preparing the outward conditions
for an easy and agreeable conversation
after dinner, an unsuitable arrangement of
furniture may act as a grave hindrance ;
and there are other arrangements which
suggest and stimulate friendly intercourse.
What these latter may be, depends on the
size and formation of the room, the temperature of the weather, and many other
circumstances. A thoughtful hostess will
see how groups of two or three can be
easily formed, and that when men come
in from dinner it may be made easy for
them to scatter, and find new topics
among new groups.

But whatever the best arrangement may
be, there can be no doubt that the ideally
worst is to set a row of chairs all round
the wall, and leave the middle of the room

perfectly bare and empty. Were it the professed object of the hostess to make it difficult or formidable for men to resume conversation with the ladies of the party, this would be her natural course to pursue. And yet this astonishing arrangement of a room is not imaginary, but real. It seems to be even common in provincial society, for I have not only heard of it, but seen it myself since this book first appeared.

In many small points the text has been revised and corrected, and some notes have been added on topics arising out of the reviews of the former edition.

TRINITY COLLEGE, DUBLIN,
April 1888.

PREFACE

TO THE FIRST EDITION

IF the reader should inquire what special claims the present author can put forward to treat so complex and indeed novel a subject, the first reply is, of course, that he has thought a long time and with much care about it, and this, for a theorist, is sufficient vindication. But it may fairly be added that a writer on the principles of conversation ought to live in a country where the practice of it is confessedly on a high level, and where the average man is able to talk well. This is an additional

b

justification. Lastly, though examples cannot teach the art, it is to be expected that the writer should not live altogether in his study, but should go out and hear as many good conversations as possible, in order to bring his theories to the practical test. These three conditions having been honestly fulfilled, the failure of the book will rather be due to want of ability than to want of honest preparation in the author.

The generality of the treatment may perhaps mislead the reader to think that there is nothing but speculation attempted. This is not so, each single case of general description being drawn from instances under the author's own observation, so that not a few will be recognised by those who have moved in the same society.

But, if justly drawn, they ought to be found in every society.

In seeking for advice among those whose conversation has supplied the best materials for his theory, the author has been fortunate enough to obtain the assistance of the MARCHIONESS OF LONDONDERRY and LADY AUDREY BULLER, who have made suggestions and criticisms which he here cordially acknowledges.

TRINITY COLLEGE, DUBLIN,
September 1887.

ANALYSIS

INTRODUCTION.

Conversation (1) is universal ;
          (2) is necessary ; and therefore
          (3) Is it an art ? (§ 2)
          (4) Can it be improved ?

The great difficulty is this : that it must seem to be natural, and not an art.   Hence—

          (5) Analogy of the arts of logic and rhetoric (§§ 3, 4), viz.—

(α) They can never be taught without natural gifts to receive them.

(β) They can always be greatly improved in those who possess these gifts.

(γ) They must not be paraded, or they cease to be arts in the higher sense, for

(δ) The highest art is to attain perfect nature.

So also—

          (1) No teaching by mere specimens and by memory is possible (§ 5).

          (2) All the general rules are obvious, and yet

          (3) Natural gifts are necessary to apply them with skill.

(2) Quality, for we speak with (α) equals (§ 40), (β) superiors (§§ 41, 42), (γ) inferiors (§§ 43), digression on bilingual societies (§ 44).

(3) Differences (A) of age (§§ 45-47), (1) older, (2) younger, (3) equal ; (B), of sex—men and women (§§ 48-50).

(4) Degrees of Intimacy, (α) relations, (β) friends, (γ) acquaintances (familiar, slight), §§ 51-53.

II. The Matter of Conversation, or

(C) The Topics, which are either—

In Quantity—infinite (§ 54).
In Quality—serious or trivial (§ 55).
In Relation—personal or general (§§ 56, 57).

(D) The handling of the Topics must be either—

Deliberative, or by all the company.
Controversial, or by two speakers.
Epideictic, or by one (§§ 58, 59).

Epilogue.

THE PRINCIPLES

OF THE

ART OF CONVERSATION

INTRODUCTION

§ 1. THERE can be no doubt that of all
the accomplishments prized in modern
society that of being agreeable in conversation is the very first. It may be
called the social result of Western
civilisation, beginning with the Greeks.
Whatever contempt the North American
Indian or the Mohammedan Tartar may
feel for talking as mere chatter, it is
agreed among us that people must meet
frequently, both men and women, and
that not only is it agreeable to talk, but
that it is a matter of common courtesy

B

to say something, even when there is
hardly anything to say. Every civilised
man and woman feels, or ought to feel,
this duty ; it is the universal accomplish-
ment which all must practise, and as
those who fail signally to attain it are
punished by the dislike or neglect of
society, so those who succeed beyond the
average receive a just reward, not only in
the constant pleasure they reap from it, but
in the esteem which they gain from their
fellows. Many men and many women
owe the whole of a great success in life
to this and nothing else.[1] An agreeable
young woman will always carry away the
palm in the long run from the most bril-

---

[1] Of course I do not mean to say that there are not
moral conditions required, the absence of which would
make social talents perfectly useless. But two men may
have equally good moral characters, and one may fail
from shyness or awkwardness, while the other succeeds,
not because he is respectable, but because he is agreeable.
If he is immoral he deserves to fail, and almost invariably
does so. If he is moral he may or may not succeed,
according as he is agreeable or not.

liant player or singer who has nothing
to say. And though men are supposed
to succeed in life by dead knowledge, or
by acquaintance with business, it is often
by their social qualities, by their agreeable
way of putting things, and not by their
more substantive merits, that they prevail.
In the high profession of diplomacy, both
home and foreign, this is pre-eminently the
case.

But quite apart from all these serious
profits, and better than them all, is the
daily pleasure derived from good conversation by those who can contribute it themselves or enjoy it in others. It is a perpetual intellectual feast, it is an ever-ready
recreation, a deep and lasting comfort,
costing no outlay but that of time,
requiring no appointments but a small
company, limited neither to any age nor
any sex, the delight of prosperity, the
solace of adversity, the eternal and essential expression of that social instinct which

is one of the strongest and best features
in human nature.[1]

§ 2. If such be the universality and the
necessity of conversation in modern society,
it seems an obvious inquiry whether it can
be taught or acquired by any fixed method ;
or rather, as everybody has to practise it
in some way, not as a mere ornament, but
as a necessity of life, it may be asked :
Is there any method by which we can
improve our conversation ?   Is there any
theory of it which we can apply in our
own case and that of others ?   If not, are
there at least some practical rules which
we ought to know, and which we should
follow in endeavouring to perform this
essential part of our social duties ?

To assert that there is some such sys-

---

1 I have explained in the new Preface why I have not
here included the profound moral uses of conversation,
which is in fact the main vehicle of good education and
of religious teaching.   But I can assure my critics that I
do not appreciate this serious side of conversation the
less because I thought it foreign to this book.

tematic analysis of conversation possible
is to assert that it is an *Art*—a practical
science like the art of reasoning called
Logic, or the art of eloquence called
Rhetoric. Now this runs counter to one
of the strongest convictions among intelligent men and women, that if anything in the world ought to be spontaneous it is conversation. How can a
thing be defined by rules which consists
in following the chances of the moment,
drifting with the temper of the company,
suiting the discourse to whatever subject
may turn up? The instant any one is
felt to be talking by rules all the charm of
his society vanishes, and he becomes the
worst of social culprits—a bore. For it is
the natural easy flow of talk, drifting with
the current of thought in its changing
eddies, which is indeed the perfection of
what we seek. Didactic teaching, humor-
ous anecdotes, clever argument — these
may take their part in social intercourse,

but they are not its real essence, as I
understand it.   To take up what others say
in easy comment, to give in return something which will please, to stimulate the
silent and the morose out of their vapours
and surprise them into good-humour, to
lead while one seems to follow—this is the
real aim of good conversation.

How can such a Protean impalpable
acquirement be in any way an art depend-
ing on rules?   Does it not altogether
depend on natural gifts, on a ready power
of expression, on a sanguine temperament,
on a quick power of sympathy, on a placid
temper?   Is there not a risk, nay a cer-
tainty, that in dissecting it we shall slay
its life and destroy its beauty?

§ 3. However natural and reasonable
this objection, it is based on the mistake
that art is opposed to nature, that natural
means *merely* what is spontaneous and unprepared, and artistic what is *manifestly*
studied and artificial.   This is one of the

commonest and most widely-spread popular errors.   If such were the real meaning of *natural*, it might be argued that
nothing was natural in man above the
condition of the lowest savage—the *Natur-
mensch*, as the Germans call him.   And if
such were the meaning of *artistic*, we must
exclude from art the highest of all its
functions—that of reproducing, or perhaps even of producing, nature in its most
precious and perfect phases.   It is a curious
reflection that conventionality and awkwardness seem our most universal inheritance, and so far thoroughly natural to
man, that we all require either conscious
art or the heedlessness attending some
violent emotion to keep us clear of it.
The savage has it strongly marked in him ;
the most enlightened societies are encum-
bered with it.   Ask any child of five or six
years old, anywhere over Europe, to draw
you the figure of a man, and it will always
produce very much the same kind of thing.

You might, therefore, assert that this was the *natural* way for a child to draw a man, and yet how remote from nature it is.   If one or two out of a thousand made a fair attempt and avoided the conventional treatment, you would attribute this either to special genius or special training—and why? because the child had really approached nature.

§ 4. Let us leave generalities and consider practical sciences, which have a closer analogy to the subject under discussion. The science of Logic or analysis of reasoning professes to show us how men ought to reason, and to discover the precise nature of their mistakes when they reason falsely. Yet the best reasoner is not the man who parades his logic and thrusts syllogisms upon his opponents, but he who states his arguments as if they arose spontaneously and followed one another by natural suggestion.   In fact, the man who parades his logic is one of those poor and narrow thinkers whose over-attention to form mars his comprehension of the matter, and so leads him astray. The formally logical reasoner is generally a bad persuader. And yet logic is not to be blamed for this man's stupidity. The fact that he goes wrong on every practical question is not due to logic, but to the man's narrowness of vision or his vanity in parading an art that does not admit of parade in its proper use.

The case is still clearer with Rhetoric, or the science of speaking persuasively in public. Here we have a science so akin to that of which we are in search, that the points of importance may serve as direct clues to discover what we seek. The most obvious points about rhetoric as a practical science are these : it pre-supposes some natural gifts in the pulpit, and though we have notable instances of men overcoming great congenital ob-stacles by study, the fact of this very

conquest shows that a fund of power or
of passion lay concealed beneath these
hindrances.   No stupid person, no person
without any flow of ideas, ever was, or
could be made, an effective speaker by
studying rhetoric.

On the other hand, every speaker, bad
or good, is greatly improved by a study
of this science, and by reflecting on the
suggestions it gives him.   There is no
orator, however naturally ready and fluent,
who will not profit immensely by such a
study.   Nay, even those who have formed
themselves as speakers by long practice,
have generally constructed for themselves
some such science or body of rules which
they consciously obey, and which gives
them most of their efficiency and power ;
so that, even if they have succeeded without studying the science of rhetoric, they
are not therefore devoid of rhetorical study.

But it is of the last importance, as was
already observed in the case of logic, that

a man's theory of speaking should not be paraded to his hearers. The moment they are made aware that he has drawn up premeditated engines of persuasion, as it were, in position, they fortify themselves against them, and what the orator gains in display he loses in power. For here, as in all art, the real perfection is to reproduce nature—not nature in its halting and stammering and repetition, but nature in its most perfect and purified form. Here, too, the untutored speaker is always conventional and consciously awkward ; it is the trained orator who is easy and graceful ; he is, in fact, at home not only with his audience, but, if I may say so, with himself.

In public speaking, however, studied effects and evident preparation, though not agreeable, though not showing the highest art, are still excusable, owing to the acknowledged difficulties with which that art is beset. It is not so with conversation.

Here, if anywhere, the first thing to be
aimed at is to appear perfectly natural.
Hence the fact that no 'theory of conversation' has yet been attempted.
But hence also the fact that such an
analysis is very much needed, and that
conversation generally is at a far lower
level than it might be.   The many analo-
gies already pointed out, and many others
which will suggest themselves to any intelligent reader, indicate that the line to
be followed in this discussion must be
determined by the sister art of rhetoric, if
indeed conversation can be called a sister
art, and not a mere pendant to the former.
In general, good public speakers are also
agreeable in conversation ; the art of per-
suading people from a platform is nearly
akin to that of pleasing them in social
discourse, though there are of course some
men only fit for the greater and more
serious mission, and some who are perfect enough in the lesser, yet who can-

not rise to the importance of the greater task.[1]

§ 5. The analogy, therefore, being established, we may feel tolerably certain of the following results, which should be stated at the outset in order to allay any vain or excessive expectations : (1) no teaching of the art of conversation by specimens is possible. Even in rhetoric this is very difficult, and yet rhetoric is busied about weighty topics which must often recur in the same form. But in the case of conversation, except to point out some notable examples in great authors, any teaching by special cases is quite illusory. It would at once tempt the learner to force the train of the discourse into the vein he

---

[1] So it was said of Phæax, the contemporary of Alcibiades and Cleon, λαλεῖν ἄριστος, ἀδυνατώτατος λέγειν—a capital talker, but the worst of speakers. Any one who has thought of comparing Englishmen with Irishmen as writers and talkers, will have observed that a brilliant and witty English writer is often dull in conversation, whereas there are Irishmen whose talk is first-rate, and their writing dull and poor.

had practised, and to force conversation is in other words to spoil it. (2) As in logic and in rhetoric, we may be certain that all the general rules, when stated, will be perfectly obvious. The notion of any of these sciences being mysteries, whereby a secret or magic power is to be acquired, is only fit for the dark ages. The broad foundations of logic are nothing but truisms ; the rules of rhetoric are founded on these truisms, combined with psychological observations neither subtle nor deep. So we may be certain that the laws of good conversation, being such as can be practised by all, are no witchery, but something simple and commonplace, perhaps neglected on account of its very plainness. (3) Simple as these rules may be, it requires a certain special faculty to apply them—a faculty which may be called common sense, or judgment, or genius—a something which some men and women have not at all, and can never acquire, but which the great majority have in some degree ; and this determines their success more than all the rules in the world. So it is with eloquence of the higher kind. What are called natural gifts start one man far ahead of another. And yet these external qualities may be outrun by a larger mental gift, which overcomes weakness of voice and poverty of frame, and makes a man whose presence is mean, and whose speech at first contemptible, fascinate great audiences with his genius. We may be unable to define what this peculiar quality is in the case of conversation, but we must take care to recognise its presence from the very outset.

SUBJECTIVE SIDE—PHYSICAL CONDITIONS

§ 6. There are no special physical conditions absolutely necessary for becoming a good talker. I have known a man with a painful impediment in his speech far more agreeable than all the fluent people in the room. But when any one comes to consider by what conditions conversation can be improved, and turns first of all to his own side, to see what he can do for himself in that direction, he will find that certain natural gifts which he may possess, or the absence of which he may regret, are of no small importance in making him more agreeable to those whom he meets in society. It seems desirable to mention these at the outset for completeness' sake, and also that educators may lay their foundations in children for after use in the world.

The old Greeks set it down as an axiom that a loud or harsh voice betokened bad breeding, and any one who hears the lower classes discussing any topic at the corners of the streets, may notice not merely their coarseness and rudeness in expression, but also the loudness and harshness of their

voices, in support of this observation. The
habit of wrangling with people who will
not listen without interruption, and who
try to shout down their company, nay even
the habit of losing one's temper, engenders
a noisy and harsh way of speaking, which
naturally causes a prejudice against the
talker in good society. Even the dog-
matic or over-confident temper which
asserts opinions loudly, and looks round to
command approval or challenge contradiction, chills good conversation by setting
people against the speaker, whom they
presume to be a social bully and wanting
in sympathy.

Contrariwise, nothing attracts more at
first hearing than a soft and sweet tone of
voice. It generally suggests a deeper well
of feeling than the speaker possesses, and
certainly prejudices people as much in his
favour as a grating or loud utterance repels
them. It is to be classed with personal
beauty, which disposes every one to favour

the speaker, and listen to him or her with
sympathy and attention.   This sweetness
in the tone of the voice is chiefly a natural
gift, but it may also be improved, if not
acquired, by constant and careful training in early years.   It can certainly be
marred by constant straining and shout-
ing.   It should therefore be carefully
cultivated or protected in youth as a
valuable vantage-ground in social intercourse.[1]

Similarly the presence of a strong local
accent, though there are cases where it
gives raciness to wit and pungency to satire,

[1] The fact that harshness of voice may be so diffused
as to become a national feature suggests that there may
be physical causes for it which are not yet ascertained.
Thus it always strikes me that Italian women speak their
beautiful language with extraordinary harshness ; and how
many witty and charming American people are noticed at
once, and with regret, for this hard and grating intonation.
The conversation of these people betrays them at a dis-
tance, and without their words being distinguished.   I
have no doubt that careful training would soften this defect,
but it seems to have some root in physique or climate.

is usually a hindrance to conversation, especially at its outset, and among strangers.[1]   It marks a man as provincial, and hence is akin to vulgarity and narrowness of mind.   It suggests too that the speaker has not moved much about the world, or even in the best society of his native country, in which such provincialism is carefully avoided, and set down as an index of mind and manners below the proper level.   Hence all careful educators endeavour to eradicate peculiarities of accent or pronunciation in children, and justly, though we have all met great talkers

[1] It has been suggested to me that a slight impediment or stammer often gives peculiar zest to conversation.   But this is hardly the case at first hearing ; it is only appreciated when we have discovered that what the speaker is hesitating to utter is worth waiting for.   It then produces the same kind of surprise that irony does, which is often deliberate mental stammering—that is to say, a man affects simplicity or hesitation who is really master of the situation, and intends his affectation to be understood as such. I add this explanation because intelligent readers found some difficulty in understanding my brief definition of irony.

whose Scotch burr or Irish brogue seemed
an essential feature of their charm.   If
this be so, no education will eradicate it.
In lesser people to be provincial is distinctly
an obstacle in the way, even though a great
mind may turn it into a stepping-stone.

§ 7. There is yet another almost physical disability or damage to conversation,
which is akin to provincialism, and which
consists in disagreeable tricks in conversation, such as the constant and meaningless
repetition of catchwords and phrases, such
as the unmeaning oaths of our grandfathers,
such as inarticulate sounds of assent, such
as contortions of the face, which so annoy
the hearer by their very want of meaning
and triviality as to excite quite a serious
dislike to the speaker, and to require great
and sterling qualities to counterbalance
this first impression.   However apt a
man's internal furniture may be for conversation, he may make it useless by
being externally disagreeable, and how

often when we praise a friend as a good
talker do we hear the reply : I should like
him well enough if he did not worry me
with his *don't you know*, or his *what*, or his
exactly so, or something else so childishly
small, that we shudder to think how easily
a man may forfeit his position or popularity
among civilised men in their daily intercourse.   But modern society, which ought
to be of all things in human life the most
easy and unconstrained, is growing every
day more tyrannical, and is now only to
be kept in good humour by careful attention to its unwritten behests, unless indeed
we have the power to bend it to our will,
and force it to follow our lead instead of
driving us along like slaves.

The effect of these trifles is like the
effect of other personal habits upon a
man's general reputation.   If he be untidy,
and neglect to wash his face or brush his
clothes, he will require very sterling virtues
to counteract the dislike which his appear-

ance creates.   On the other hand, if a man
or woman be overdressed, and ostentatiously
neat, the public at once infers triviality or
shallowness of character ; and such a person
will find difficulty in proving that he has
serious views of life, and is trustworthy in
the conduct of weighty affairs.

No more need be said concerning these
physical conditions, which are rather
negative conditions, or fávourable starting
points, than real aids for our purpose. The
handsomest man or woman, even with the
sweetest tones of human voice, will soon be
found out, if dull or unsympathetic, and then
these advantages all go for nothing.

MENTAL CONDITIONS—SPECIAL KNOWLEDGE

§ 8. Far more important than the
physical gifts of nature, which can only
be slightly improved, though they can be
completely marred, by habit, are the mental

conditions of conversation.   Among these
the most obvious is, of course, Knowledge.
A man's ignorance can never make him
agreeable in conversation, except as a butt ;
a man full of knowledge is certain to
be agreeable if he will conform to the
other conditions of the game.   The word
knowledge is, however, so vague, that we
must be at pains to define more particularly its meanings, and consider what kind
of knowledge is most conducive to good
conversation.

Of course the first question suggested
to the reader is whether general or special
knowledge in a talker is to be preferred.
There are arguments in favour of each.
Let us take the specialist first.   There is
undoubtedly a great satisfaction in talking
to a man who is master of any special subject, even if it be remote from ordinary life.
Intelligent questions will draw from the
astronomer, from the chemist, possibly
from the pure mathematician, curious facts

and interesting views on the progress of discovery, which will pleasantly beguile the time even in a light-minded and frivolous company.   This opens a field for conversation which is inaccessible if there be no one present to explain or to speak with authority, and so no invitation is more frequent or more welcome than to come and meet a man celebrated in his own line and of wide reputation.   The very fact of meeting such a man disposes the company to be sympathetic, and to draw from him the secrets of his knowledge.

This kind of vantage-ground may be occupied by a man of no original capacity or deep learning, if accident has made him intimate with some exciting or absorbing subject of the day.   The man who has just escaped a shipwreck, or fought in a famous battle, or survived some catastrophe, has for the moment the advantage of being endowed with special knowledge, which everybody wants to talk about, and

to learn particulars from the actual eye-
witness.   Akin to this is the advantage of
having seen and conversed with the greatest
men of the day—a feature which lends
the principal charm to those volumes of
autobiography or of *Recollections*, which
approach nearer than any other kind
of book to the conditions of a mere conversation.

§ 9. Of course the danger with either of
these specialists, the specialist of a day or
the specialist of years, is that he will not
leave his subject when it has been sufficiently discussed, as he will probably gauge
the interest of others by his own preoccupation, and so may become not a blessing
but a bore to his company.   Though this
is frequently the case, those who have
gathered company about them for conversation, and have long experience of what
is most likely to succeed, will agree with
me that to have a specialist present is
always valuable.   If other topics flag an

appeal to this abundant source will always introduce a new current of talk, and often of the most agreeable kind.

Neither of these mental conditions, which are distinctly valuable in society, includes the case of specialists on topics which are of no universal or no perman-ent interest. Thus there are in English society men devoted to one particular sport or one narrow pursuit, upon which they can talk with authority indeed, and with interest, but only to those who have received the same training. A party of fox-hunters, or racing-men, or college dons, or stockbrokers, who rehearse again in the evening what they have been doing all day, may indeed amuse themselves with talk, but in no sense is it good con-versation.[1]   One specialist, as I have said,

[1] As this book has been accused of excessive worldli-ness, I will add here a moral reflection. The habit of constantly talking over the events of the day not only makes men narrow and uninteresting, it leads them to exaggerate to themselves the importance and dignity of

may be of the greatest use in conversation.
A set of specialists when they get together
are either unintelligible to the average mind
or exceedingly tedious.

The same remarks apply to specialists,
men or women, who can only discuss
topics interesting to one sex. I will not
go so far as to say that no conversation
can be first-rate which does not include
speakers of both sexes ; the divergence
in the education and the life of our boys
and of our girls is still too wide to make

their work, or even their amusement. Recent events
in Ireland have shown that a set of fox-hunters can talk
themselves into a moral attitude at total variance with
personal honour and public spirit. The dishonest casu-
istry by which they seek to justify themselves can be
attained even by dull country gentlemen, if they talk a
matter over long enough among themselves. In the
most recent case, the arguments were suggested by
cleverer people—horse-dealers, whose object was mere
gain ; and rich tradespeople, who know no responsibility
beyond getting amusement for their outlay of money.
But gentlemen can only have persuaded themselves to
adopt such arguments by the constant encouragement of
long conversations over their wine.

such a limitation reasonable. But it is surely a bad sign of any society to find men's parties considered more agreeable than those of both sexes, for it is a sign either of licence in men's talk or of narrowness in women's education. There are cases of both within most people's experience. The latter is notably the case in some parts of Ireland, and arises from the want of *political* education in Irish women of any but the highest classes. And so it is in many other countries. But this is verging upon the educational conclusions, which we must postpone to another occasion.

GENERAL KNOWLEDGE

§ 10. We come now to the broader condition of General Knowledge. This, in the minds of many, sums up in itself all the conditions of good conversation, and

yet to assert it is so partial a truth as to
be practically misleading.   A great mistake lies at the root of such an opinion,
which assumes that the first object of
conversation is not to please but to instruct.[1]   I could produce one hundred
Irish peasants more agreeable than many
a highly-informed Englishman, and yet
these peasants might in many cases be
unable to read or write.   Of course to
instruct or to be instructed is often very
pleasant, and so far knowledge, general or
special, is a very useful help to conversation, but it is as talk, not as a lesson, that
we must here regard it.

The advantage of general above special
knowledge for our purpose is that it can
be applied in a greater number of cases,
and used to interest a greater number of
people.   The man of general knowledge

---

[1] This proposition, which should perhaps have been
formally stated at the outset, is now explained and
defended in the new Preface to this edition.

can suit himself to various company, and, if he is not able to speak with the authority of the specialist, can at least help and stimulate in many cases where the latter is likely to be silent. If therefore we exclude the object of gaining information, which many people estimate, not, indeed, above its intrinsic importance, but above its importance in conversation, regarded not as a lesson, but a recreation, we must decide that general information is the better condition to promote agreeable social intercourse.

It may be attained in two directions ; either by the knowledge of books or the knowledge of men. The former is within the reach of most men, even though it requires a peculiar memory to make it applicable with ease and readiness. We may even say with truth that no man can attain to general knowledge nowadays without reading many books. The danger of a desultory habit, very likely to arise from skimming the mass of ephemeral literature now gushing from the press is, that the facts acquired will not be set in order, and will come out as untidy scraps, not as the details of a proper system of study. The books which a man reads may either be the great masters, which are perhaps rather useful for cultivating his deeper self than for ordinary converse, or the newest authors, whose merits are still upon trial, and who therefore afford an excellent field for discussion and criticism. But there is hardly a distinction to be drawn between the specialist in great books and the generalist in many, for all people are supposed to study literature in general, and a good knowledge of either familiar or fashionable books can hardly fail to tell in any gathering of cultivated men and women.

§ 11. There is, however, another kind of general knowledge which is not so easy to acquire, for it requires long experience,

a certain position in society, and means
for foreign travel. I mean the general
knowledge of remarkable men, concerning
whom the speaker can tell his recollections. There is often a man of no great
learning or ability whose official position,
tact, or private means have brought him
into relation with the great minds about
whom every detail is interesting. Such a
man's general knowledge should always
make him an agreeable member of society.
Akin to this man is the experienced
traveller who has wandered through many
lands and seen the cities and the ways of
men. The peculiar advantage of this
kind of general knowledge for conversation is that its very acquisition comes in
the practice of society, and that all those
defects of narrowness, awkwardness, and
self-consciousness which often mar the
man of books, are rubbed off, as the
phrase is, by constant friction with various
men. The man of books, on the contrary,

has to acquire his store in the silence of his study, and hence by a process which rather untrains him for talking, so that even though his knowledge when acquired may be of more solid and permanent value, his way of producing it may put him at a disadvantage.

Let me add before leaving this head that the enormous increase of the means for acquiring knowledge, and the application of great inventions to save time in so doing, are by no means accompanied by corresponding strides in the art of conversation. All the knowledge of the day professes to be curtailed and collected into newspapers, periodicals, and handbooks, just as all the travelling of the day is done by rail and steam, with the aid of guide-books, which save the traveller all the trouble and all the education of thinking. The tourist who formerly went through Italy with his *vetturino*, and saw every village and road deliberately, talking

D

with the people and observing national
life, is now whirled through tunnels and
by night from one capital to another,
where he sees what Cook or Murray
chooses him to see, just as the man who
trusts the newspapers for his knowledge
gets scraps, perversions, even lies, served
up for him by way of universal information.   It is easy to see that this kind of
training, as it interferes with both liberty
and leisure of thought, and induces men
to spend far too much time in gathering
materials, is in no way conducive to the
improvement of conversation.

INTELLECTUAL QUICKNESS

§ 12. What has hitherto been said
about knowledge in a man of conversation has left out of all account the way
of producing it, and merely considered
the mental store from which conversation

may be supplied. But almost as important as these materials, is the faculty of producing them without effort. This quality may be called intellectual *quickness*, as distinguished from solidity ; and of all the conditions we have yet discussed, this seems most due to nature, and unattainable by education. It is indeed sometimes a characteristic of nations. The Irishman or the Frenchman will show this quality with an average excellence far above that attained in England or Germany. It may of course be allied with, or even due to, some such moral quality as sympathy, of which we shall speak presently. But quite apart from moral goodness, a selfish man, who has no sympathy for his company, may, by the quickness of his intellect, show brilliantly in conversation, while his more solid and worthy fellow is considered a bore.

As I have just said, this brightness

is generally a gift of nature. Some men and some nations are born with quick wits. But even so it is a great mistake to think that it may not be vastly improved by intercourse with people who have the faculty already well developed. Moreover, it is a very dangerous advantage, and if not deepened by solid acquirements, or chastened by moral restraints, may make a man rather the scourge than the delight of his company.

For this is the mental quality which is the foundation of wit, and a joker who merely consults his own amusement, or the amusement of some of his hearers at the expense of others, is not a good converser. The tendency of a very quick intellect is also akin to impatience, and so it will interfere with and cow more modest minds, which might have contributed well to the feast of talk had they been allowed to work without hurry or pressure. So strong do we often find this contrast that

it is unadvisable, in choosing a set of
people for conversation, to bring together
very slow and very quick intellects.
While the former are more dazzled and
confused than pleased, the latter feel the
delay of listening to long and deliberate
sentences intolerable; and so a company
in which all the members are socially excellent may fail to be pleasant on account
of the mental contrasts of its members.

Let me illustrate it by an extreme case.
Who would think of introducing a young
brilliant flashing sceptic into a society of
grave and sober orthodoxy? If the conversation did not soon degenerate into acrid
controversy—the very lees of social intercourse—it would result in contemptuous
silence on one side or other, probably with
the contempt so transparent as to challenge harsh over-statement from the talker
by way of challenge or reply to unspoken
censure. Could anything be more ruinous
to the object we have in view? It may

be urged on the other hand that if too many
quick intellects are brought together—not
a very easy thing, by the way, to accomplish—the pressure will become too great
and the conversation move so fast that the
strain may become a weariness.   I think
that any danger in this direction is rather
due to the moral defects of the talkers
than their intellectual brightness, and so
I shall discuss this point under another
head.

But if the quality under consideration
is valuable at all times, it is so pecu-
liarly when a number of strangers meet
together, or when it is the lot of men and
women to be obliged to talk together in
dialogue, upon a stray or sudden occasion.   Then it is, when for example you
go down to dinner with a strange man or
woman whose name you have not caught,
that quickness of intellect becomes the
prime agent in starting a pleasant conversation.   There are, indeed, even here

many easy rules which may help to get
over the initial difficulty, without those
initial chords about the weather whereby
so many people, otherwise really intelligent, hide themselves at the outset under
the prelude of commonplace.[1]   But here
as elsewhere art can only imitate better
nature.

It is further to be added that as knowledge, both general and special, is princi-
pally to be expected from men, so quickness of mind, which is often impaired by
deeper study, is the proper attribute of
women, and ought to be the distinctive
quality of their conversation.   This is
supposed to be so in French society; I
cannot say that it has come under my
observation as a general law, the many
instances which I have met being always

[1] I have been charged with speaking disrespectfully of
the weather, that old and well tried subject of conversation.   I am certain that the common sense of mankind
has justly fixed upon it as a prelude, but only as a suitable prelude when nothing better suggests itself.

noted and quoted as brilliant and as exceptional, so implying that it was not the rule.

Moral Conditions—Modesty

§ 13. We may now pass from the intellectual conditions of conversation to
what I may call, for simplicity's sake, the
moral conditions.   It is, of course, certain
that these so-called moral qualities are
frequently congenital or constitutional, and
that, therefore, the owner of them deserves
no credit for possessing them.   But as
they are qualities enjoined upon us by
moralists, and are in any case analogous
to moral virtues, we may in this book,
which does not affect precise philosophy,
class them as moral.   For example, the
instinct of sociality, which is really the
same as the gregarious instinct in birds
and animals, is not the same as the love
of our neighbour enjoined by the Gospel,
but is closely connected with it, for to be

social without being civil is not possible,
and civility is at least the imitation of
friendship, if it be not friendship or benevolence in outward acts of social intercourse.   This, too, appears to be the reason
why a particular class of social instincts
is so agreeable to men, and so honoured
in society—their close relationship to moral
virtues.

Let me take up the first and most
obvious—Modesty.[1]   It is quite certain
that modesty and its opposite are congenital to various people.   Those who
have to do with the education of children
can see it within the limits of a family, not
to say a school.   Some boys and girls are
naturally retiring, and think little of their
powers ; others are the reverse.   But here
too, as we all know, early education may

---

[1] I include here under the word all its various grada-
tions, from mere bashfulness to that moral self-restraint
which makes us fear to assert ourselves, lest we should
imply an over-estimate of our powers.

make great changes.   A child not originally remarkable in either way may be
unduly brought forward and applauded,
or again unduly repressed and cowed,
so that the constant habit of early years
may actually modify the original character
in either of two opposite directions.   But
this is only possible when the original
nature is not strongly declared ; if it
be so, I hold the educator to be almost
helpless.

When the child is growing to maturity
it is likely to be strongly affected by
watching the defects of others, or hearing
the frequent censure of them.   Thus I see
that the children of people with too much
manner are apt to have no manner at all
(as the phrase is), and the children of
incessant talkers are so bored with this
social vice that they never think of practising talk during the absence of their
parents.   Let us apply these remarks to
modesty.

§ 14. There is no quality in man, still more in woman, which is more attractive and which commands more respect. Every intelligent and sympathetic person makes allowance for it, and strives to lessen the necessary pains which it inflicts upon the possessor of it in society. It is akin to simplicity and honesty, and opposed to that artificiality which is the outward and visible sign of some kind of dishonesty. It lends a charm to youth and inexperience, so that people who are wearied with the labours of talking to worn and world-stained equals feel, as it were, the breath of gorse and heather after the odours of city air when they come in contact with genuine modesty. It is a quality sometimes allied with that heaven-born genius which attains great results without apparent effort, and, therefore, is not infected with the pride of having gained conscious and hard-fought successes. It is, lastly, the outcome of great and solid labour, which teaches the specialist how much he fails to know, and the general student how small a fragment of human knowledge he has compassed.   Here it is no natural quality, but an acquired virtue ; yet it excites the same kind of feeling in society.

There is, therefore, no quality more highly valuable in society and more certain, *within limits*, to conduce to agreeable conversation.   Perhaps the clearest reservation, and one which will cover almost all the various cases, is this : *modesty without simplicity*, though it may still be a moral virtue, is always a social vice, and therefore highly detrimental to good conversation ; for as soon as modesty becomes conscious, it assumes one of two forms—the parade of apology or the cloak of reserve.

I need hardly insist that the man or woman who displays modesty by constantly apologising for native ignorance

or stupidity injures conversation, and can
only amuse a company by becoming
ridiculous. What we want to learn from
each member is his free opinion on
the subject in hand, not his own estimate of the value of that opinion.
How evidently this is a social vice will
appear from the fact that an assumption
of this kind of modesty is one of the
commonest and most diverting forms of
humour—I mean the irony which has
been the helper of conversation ever since
the days of Socrates, as we find him in
Plato's *Dialogues*.

MORAL CONDITIONS—SIMPLICITY

§ 15. We cannot analyse the second
form of conscious modesty, Reserve, till we
have said a few words on the virtue akin
to modesty which reserve particularly vio-
lates, I mean the quality of Simplicity.
It is a great mistake to say that sim-

plicity as such is always a virtue.   There
is, for example, the *enfant terrible*, who
upsets everybody and causes shocking
shame and confusion by the indiscreet
directness of his inquiries.   The very same
kind of mistake is made by grown people
who are ignorant of the ways of society,
such as country girls, or girls of an inferior
rank, who are married into a cultivated
society, and who are allowed such liber-
ties, either for their beauty's sake, or for
novelty's sake, that they announce whatever comes into their head, and disturb
conversation by their irrelevancy and
shallowness, if not by suggesting subjects undesirable in general society.
There is also the blunt man, whose simplicity takes the form of rudeness, who
thinks it more important that he should
speak out the plain truth than that he
should spare the feelings of others.   This
is again a vice parading under the form
of a virtue—perhaps here of truthfulness

rather than simplicity, but the two are
so akin that at this point we need not
draw distinctions. The conversational side
of truthfulness is after all little more than
directness and simplicity of utterance.

So far then I have put the defects of
simplicity first, because they are more
likely to be overlooked than its advantages.
When, therefore, these important limitations are made, and they affect a great
number of cases, we must admit that there
is the greatest charm in simplicity, in
the temper which, without assumption of
ignorance or parade of inexperience, opens
a candid eye of inquiry upon the company,
receives with readiness new information,
and is willing to tell without conceits or
ornaments the actual impressions in the
speaker's mind.

It may be found not only along with
genius, which is often of this character, but
along with mere experience and acuteness ;
we hear, for example, that it is the lead-

ing characteristic of Prince Bismarck's conversation ; it was so likewise, as I well remember, in the conversation of the late Isaac Butt, an Irish genius of the highest order, and a talker second to none, whose life was stormy, and whose character not by any means such as would naturally imply this quality of simplicity.

On the other hand, it is quite extravagant to postulate it as a necessary sign of genius, and to say that those who are wanting in it are certainly wanting either in ability or honesty. For there are great minds naturally wanting in simplicity, just as there are great minds wanting in modesty or in truthfulness—such as J. J. Rousseau and the great Napoleon in the latter two, and one great English writer of our day in the former, whom I need not name. Human nature will not be tied down in any such fetters.

But when all has been said that can be said on either side, it will remain certain that the man who appears simple, and who therefore affects his company with the impression that they are in direct contact with his mind, has a distinct advantage over those who, either from conceits of style, or over-delicacy of sentiment, or education in an artificial atmosphere, appear with their minds as it were dressed or tattooed, and not in the purity of nature.

I need hardly add that it is necessary to sever simplicity from modesty as social qualities, since the one may even contradict the other, though they are so often in harmony. The blunt man above mentioned, who speaks out his mind with over-simplicity, may be very devoid of modesty ; and, conversely, there are certain phases of modesty, such as *prudery*, which make the speaker avoid simplicity, and cover his meaning by various subterfuges. It is when the two qualities work together, and appear habitual to the speaker, that

E

they produce their admirable effect. If
he is narrating, for example, a tragic
history, or story of adventure in which
he has taken part, while modesty will
prevent him from magnifying his own
share in the matter, and so trying to the
utmost the faith of his hearers, simplicity
will prevent him from unduly concealing
his action, and will ensure that he tells
the whole truth, so far as he knows it.
If, again, he be asked his opinion on a
question which he has studied, and upon
which he ought to be an authority, his
modesty may prevent him from giving the
company the benefit of his knowledge,
unless his simplicity makes him attend
directly to the matter in hand, and not to
the position of referee in which he suddenly comes to be placed.

Moral Conditions—Shyness, Reserve

§ 16. We have kept till now the main violation of simplicity, and greatest of modern hindrances to conversation, which we have already mentioned in connection with modesty.

What distinction are we to make between Shyness and Reserve, two qualities whose effects are generally similar, and each of which is a great hindrance to good conversation? We may start from the distinctions in ordinary use. No man or woman will openly claim to be reserved, but many will plead that they are shy. The reason of this is that shyness is assumed to be a physical or at least constitutional thing, whereas reserve implies deliberate choice to stand aloof, and repel any intimacy of conversation as unwarranted either

by the circumstances or by the relative
position of the speakers. Thus though
reserve *may* arise from modesty, it is
generally a form of pride, which for that
reason no one will attribute to himself.[1]
On the other hand shyness is either
assumed to be a form, or an excess,
of modesty, which is a virtue, or it is
assumed to be congenital, and therefore
a defect to be excused rather than a fault
to be censured. So shy people as a rule
rather 'fancy themselves'; for though
they urge their peculiarity as an excuse
for social defects, there lies deeper a secret

---

[1] I am reminded that there are, especially in England,
people who desire to be thought reserved, and are
secretly proud of this reputation. It is, of course, part of
this pride not to declare it publicly. These exceptional
cases are, however, to be classed with those of people
who are secretly proud of other vices, and do not disturb
my theory. I have even known a man who was not only
rude, but so proud of his rudeness, that he solicited an
appointment the duties of which consist in civility. Such
a case cannot be classed or discussed, but must simply
be set down among the unnatural vices, fortunately rare
and sporadic, in the human race.

conviction that they at least have escaped
the vice of forwardness, or of that coarseness of mental fibre which is implied in
forwardness. Accordingly, though there
are many people who sincerely regret
their shyness upon particular occasions,
as, for example, when they are compelled
to make a speech, or entertain some great
personage, yet you will not find very many
who would exchange it as a permanent
quality for perfect ease, or assurance, or
total absence of nervousness, or whatever
else the opposite of shyness may be called.
The more we reflect on this and other
similar symptoms in shyness, the more we
shall be convinced that here we have not,
as a rule, to deal with mere modesty, but
with conscious modesty; with modesty without simplicity, and therefore really with a
subtle form of conceit.[1]

---

[1] I never denied that there was such a thing as congenital and insuperable shyness in some worthy people,
which they themselves honestly regard as a real affliction ;

§ 17. There are of course cases of children who are allowed to run away whenever a stranger appears, as if nature were a state of war, and man the natural enemy of man. Such children will require training to be cured of their own and their parents' stupidity, and must be taught that every stranger is not a bogy. But this is mere domestication, such as we apply to the lower animals. It is also possible, though rare, that some people of refinement and culture may have a physical repugnance to meeting any but their intimates, and that they may make honest efforts in vain to overcome this stubborn nervousness. The great majority of shy people are not of this kind. Thus you will see a girl extremely shy in ordinary society, who blossoms out when · she receives attentions from some one who

but if my observation of human nature is correct, these cases of shyness are not more than five per cent. The rest are caused by bad education and hidden vanity.

may possibly marry her. Or else you
may find a youth, who jumps over a
hedge to avoid meeting a party of
his acquaintances on a country road,
anything but modest in lower society,
thus showing that it is a consciousness
of unfitness for good company and a
fear of being criticised which dominate him. In almost all the cases which
occur there is therefore modesty without
simplicity, a conscious and almost guilty
air ; it is often nothing better than vanity,
which fears the results of conversation ;
which desires to be thought well of, and
which from mistrust of itself puts on the
garb of modesty.

If shyness really arises from this cause
it is distinctly a moral fault. But in any
case it is socially little short of a vice. How
can any conversation be easy and natural,
how can it range from topic to topic, and
bring out the tempers and the characters
of the speakers, if any of them displays

this vice by dogged silence, by conscious
blushing when any personal topic arises, or
by the awkwardness which always accom-
panies this preoccupation with one's self?
If then the capital conditions of pleasant
intercourse are modesty and simplicity,
this defect, which always contradicts the
latter, and generally both of them, is to
be regarded as the most prevalent and
injurious anti-social vice.   The only high
quality which may be concealed, or
perhaps even displayed by shyness, is a
delicate sensitiveness, which shy people
generally postulate in themselves, but
which has far better and nobler ways of
affecting society than by impeding conversation.

§ 18. Reserve, which few venture to
claim for themselves, is a far higher and
better feeling, for it implies that the un-
willingness to enter upon conversation
arises from some deliberate judgment as
to the relative positions of the speaker

and his company—often a correct judgment, saving us from the vice of familiarity, which in an inferior is offensive, in
a superior uncomfortable, in either case
distinctly vulgar. We feel that reserve
can be laid aside in pleasant moments, and
among congenial people, and that there is
often force as well as dignity behind it.
But it is rarely a virtue which improves
conversation, and therefore need not occupy
us here. It may indeed act as a check
on licence, and so by bringing the company back from some aberration, start it
afresh on nobler and pleasanter topics.
This is so indirect a mode of action, and
may be so much more easily attained in
other ways, that I need only mention it
here for completeness' sake.

UNSELFISHNESS

§ 19. Next to modesty and simplicity
I class the moral virtue of *unselfishness.*

It is very characteristic that we have no
other word for this noble quality than the
mere negation of its opposite—the most
prevalent vice in the world.   Why can we
not describe it better?   Because in particular connections it has other names
—loyalty, devotion, self-sacrifice, which
occupy a part of the ground with more
especial attributes.   We are not here con-
cerned with these heights of human nature,
with the nobility of grand and pathetic
moments.   What shows itself in these as
devotion and self-sacrifice bears in our
commonplace life a negative and non-
descriptive name, and is yet a very distinct and valuable quality, distinct from
simplicity, distinct even from sympathy,
with which it is so often allied; it may
display itself in all kinds of men and
women who take part in a conversation.
It is not less important to the silent man
than to the talkative man, though the
latter case is the more obvious.   The

good talker who monopolises conversation,
who insists on keeping other people waiting that he may finish his story, who tells
anecdotes which are evidently unpleasant
to some of the company, but will not
forego his joke for the sake of others—the
social bully who makes butts of the more
retiring, and sallies at their expense, is
the most obvious case of a man failing
from selfishness, and losing the great
natural advantages he possesses, through
want of the opposite quality.   This is the
man too who interrupts others, who refuses
to exercise for a moment that patience
which he so often exacts.

I set down these people as failures,
and such they really are, in the truest and
highest sense, for they certainly kill more
conversation than they create, nor do they
understand that the very meaning of the
word implies a contribution-feast, an *eranos*,
as the Greeks would say, not the entertainment provided by a single host.   But

alas ! in a lesser and looser sense these
people often dominate society for years,
and are even sought out as social con-
veniences, who will keep things going at
a dinner table, and supply the defects of
silence and dulness so painfully common
in English more than in other societies.
But the punishment of the selfish talker
is sure to come at last, when he lives till
his vivacity and his power of acquiring
new things fail, while he still presumes
on his old reputation. He is then discovered to be an intolerable bore ; which,
indeed, from a higher point of view, was
always the case ; and thereupon society,
which is as selfish as he is, and insists on
being amused at all costs, throws him
aside with contempt. He has perhaps
still one place of refuge ; he may become
a high priest in that great modern temple
of selfishness—his club ; but even there
his popularity has waned, and he sinks
into that old age unfriended and unsociable

—ἄφιλον ἀπροσόμιλον—which Sophocles
regarded as one of the tragic features in
the life of man.

§ 20. I turn now to a far more common, but less observed and less censured case of social selfishness, which
requires urgently to be brought into
the light of criticism.   No man requires
to practise unselfishness more than the
silent man ; for as everybody is able
to contribute and ought to contribute
something, so the man who thrusts himself into society to enjoy the talk of
others, and will take no trouble to help, to
suggest, or to encourage, is really a serious
offender.   I have known a person of good
position, and not the least wanting in
brains, who would insist in sitting at dinner
between the two most agreeable people in
the room, in order that he might eat and
listen, while under no circumstances would
he make the smallest effort to entertain in
return.   These silent people not only take

all they can get in society for nothing, but they take it without the smallest gratitude, and have the audacity afterwards to censure those who have laboured for their amusement.

I ask the reader's pardon for illustrating this important fact by a personal anecdote. In a country house where I was staying, the host had invited the colonel commanding a neighbouring depôt and his wife to dinner, and the conversation was flagging seriously. Some mention of New Zealand in that day's papers suggested it as a topic, upon which a couple of us brought out all we knew about New Zealand, discussed the natives, then savages generally, and so restored the fortunes of the evening. The colonel and his wife still sat silent. When they were gone we said to the host that we thought it very hard work to entertain people who would not say anything to anybody. He replied that they *had* said something as they got into their

carriage.   What was it?   The colonel
observed that it was very impertinent of
people to talk about countries they had
never seen, especially in presence of a man
like himself, who had not only lived for
years in New Zealand, but had written a
book about it!   This was the thanks we
got.

§ 21. There is another special scope
for unselfishness in society, which may
fitly find its place here.   In every company there may be people either socially
or intellectually inferior to the rest, who
feel themselves somewhat *out of it* (to
use a vulgar phrase), and whom the selfish man, the big talker, the ambitious
man, is apt to ignore.   And yet these
very people may be in possession of
knowledge or of mental qualities which
will be of the highest value in conversation.   It requires unselfishness to watch
them, to appeal to their sympathies, to
draw them into the stream, and make

them feel that instead of being outsiders they are really among people anxious to know what they think and to hear what they have to say. Many a time have I seen an unknown and obscure person drawn out in this way become the leading feature in a delightful evening ; for fresh and curious knowledge, which suddenly springs from an unexpected source, can hardly fail to be profoundly interesting, and to stimulate all the active minds that hear it. Thus I remember a stupid young man successfully probed by an intelligent person, till it accidentally came out that he knew all about the wild cattle in Lord Tankerville's park (Chillingham Forest). From that moment he took the lead in the conversation, and excited a most interesting discussion, in which several very dull country farmers took an animated interest.

All this can be done by mere intellectual unselfishness, by the man or woman

who considers that each person in a
society should be attended to, and if
possible compelled to contribute to the
general entertainment. But it is both
rare to find this kind of unselfishness and difficult to apply it without
the subsidiary faculty or constitution
of mind, which many think the whole
root of good conversation—I mean
sympathy.

SYMPATHY

§ 22. The great Adam Smith, in a
book he called *Moral Sentiments*, which he
seems to have thought out as a sort of
antidote to the selfishness of the *Wealth
of Nations*,[1] managed to deduce all the
virtues from this one root of Sympathy.
Starting from the fact that man is a

---

[1] Cf. on the relation of these two books, the highly
interesting passage in H. T. Buckle's chapter on the
development of the Scotch intellect, in his famous
History of Civilisation.

gregarious animal, with social instincts, he showed that the desire to be in sympathy with our fellow-creatures, and so command their love and respect, made us watch them, consider what they felt about us, and avoid everything which might shock or hurt their opinions or their feelings.   It was this indefinite and impersonal public opinion which was by degrees made a part of ourselves, and under the name of conscience was set up as 'a man within the breast' of each of us to approve and disapprove even our most secret actions.

I quote this once famous theory here, to show how a great thinker, probably the greatest of his age, estimated the force and influence of sympathy ; and whatever exaggerations he may have made concerning it in the province of morals, it seems hard to over-estimate it in the province of social intercourse.   The first condition of any conversation at all is, that people should have their minds so far in sympathy that they are willing to talk upon the same subject, and to hear what each member of the company thinks about it. The higher condition which now comes before us is, that the speaker, apart from the matter of the conversation, feels an interest in his hearers as distinct persons, whose opinions and feelings he desires to know.

This is the real secret of the power of personal beauty in society. Only a very small number of people will fall in love with each beautiful man or woman. But nearly every one will be so far attracted by beauty that he will pay attention to what the beautiful person says, and feel a keen interest to know what mind and temper accompany such perfection of form. Thus personal beauty secures the sympathy of any company; so much so, that even when found out to be a mere shell, with no mental force behind it, the attraction lasts, and lends some charm to what would otherwise be called trivial and stupid. This natural sympathy with beauty of external form is a sort of symbol of the feeling which seeks for any mental beauty or advantage to be found in a company, and by showing an interest in it, disposes the possessor of it to expand and become friendly in response to such appreciation. The sympathetic man will feel that his company talk best about the things they know best, or have had special opportunities of learning, and he will be naturally anxious to find the best side of them, and to exhibit it by his suggestions. And as in every conversation there must not only be good talking but good listening, the intellectual gifts which make the talker are often marred if he has not the sympathy which makes the listener.

This remark suggests that the social virtues of the sexes are broadly distinguished by some such principle. Women

ought not to be obliged to lead in a conversation, but it will grow dry and dull
if they are not ready with their sympathy
to hear what is said with pleasure, and to
stimulate others by quick and intelligent
appreciation. I have known a clever
woman maintain a deservedly high character for her conversation who really said
very little, but was so sympathetic that she
made her guests eloquent, and thus so
thoroughly pleased with themselves, that
she was lit up by the glow of their satisfaction, and earned very justly the credit
for talking well simply because she made
others talk. There is probably no social
talent higher than this—or rarer. There
is even a special virtue consisting in sympathetic silence, which is very different
from the selfish silence already described.
It was said with truth that no man is
really worth having as a companion with
whom you could not contentedly walk
or stay in silence. This is of course a sign

of close intimacy, and perfect freedom on both sides to meditate apart, even when together, without giving or taking any offence. Among real friends silence is no sign of estrangement, and it secures that the conversation which arises is perfectly spontaneous, which is, alas! impossible, if we are in the society of mere acquaintances who will construe our silence as rudeness.

Sympathy therefore contributes both directly and indirectly to the good of social intercourse.

§ 23. But I suppose no one will be disposed to dispute this, or to underrate the value of sympathy as a quality for conversation. It is much more likely that people may think to simplify the whole matter by arguing that, with the postulate of some brains and some education, all that is required is sympathy, and the more of it the better, so that nothing else remains to be said. We must therefore consider carefully how far this is true,

and whether there be not some important
limitations which complicate the question.

There is one on the very surface. Sympathy must not be excessive in quality,
which makes it demonstrative, and therefore likely to repel its object. We have
an excellent word which describes the
over-sympathetic person, and marks the
judgment of society, when we say that
he or she is *gushing*. Of course as
women are more frequently endowed
with this virtue than men, they also err
more frequently in the excess, at least in
Teutonic races, for among Latin races a
gushing man is quite a common pheno-
menon. This sort of person not only
volunteers to show his sympathy before it
is required, and often spoils conversation
at the outset, but is ever ready to agree
with everybody, so making discussion,
which implies differences in opinion, impossible. There results a social impression of a mixed kind, which is even more

disagreeable than downright dislike, and
therefore socially worse—I mean that of
feeling a dislike, and even something like
contempt, for a person who is known to
be full of goodness and benevolence.
Many people resent being obliged to
confuse their judgment in this way, and
feel a stronger antipathy to this marred
goodness than to proclaimed evil.

In the next place, sympathy must not
be excessive in quantity or indiscriminate,
otherwise it ceases to have any great
social value. The easiest, but also the
shallowest way of conveying your sympathy to another is to join with him in
some strong antipathy, thus showing that
all the world cannot claim your friendship,
but that you distribute your likes and dis-
likes with judgment and discrimination.
A man who is known to have a special
sympathy for some particular age or sex
or class in society is far more agreeable
to that class than he who embraces all

the world in his affections. Nay, if one usually reserved or shy expands for once, or to some few people, in contrast to his usual habit, this sympathy is indeed treasured as a real token of confidence.

These and many similar observations, which will occur to the intelligent reader, will indicate how important are the limitations of sympathy, and how essential it is that this, like every other social virtue, should be carefully husbanded, and not squandered at random without regard to its value. I should add that the foregoing remarks are specially applicable to English (I do not mean English-speaking) society. There is no people more distant and reserved in social intercourse, or that more resents any display of feeling, especially of sympathy, without a careful introduction of it, and without considerable intimacy among the company. Thus those who are accustomed to freer and more outspoken societies, not to say French and

Italian life, may make social mistakes in England on the score of sympathy, which are sins only in the heavy atmosphere of Anglo-Saxon manners.

MORAL CONDITIONS—TACT

§ 24. The highest and best of all the moral conditions for conversation is what we call *tact*. I say a condition, for it is very doubtful whether it can be called a single and separate quality; more probably it is a combination of intellectual quickness with lively sympathy. But so clearly is it an intellectual quality, that of all others it can be greatly improved, if not actually acquired, by long experience in society. Like all social excellences it is almost given as a present to some people, while others with all possible labour never acquire it. As in billiard-playing, shooting, cricket, and all these other facilities which are partly mental

and partly physical, so in tact many
never can pass a certain point of medi-
ocrity ; but still, in all these accomplishments, even those who have the talent
must practise it, and only become really
distinguished through hard work.   So it
is in art.   Music and painting are not to
be attained by the crowd.   Not even the
just criticism of these arts is attainable
without certain natural gifts ; but a great
deal of practice in good galleries and
at good concerts, and years spent among
artists, will do much to make even moder-
ately-endowed people sound judges of
excellence.

Tact, which is the sure and quick judgment of what is suitable and agreeable in
society, is likewise one of those delicate
and subtle qualities, or a combination of
qualities, which is not very easily defined,
and therefore not teachable by fixed
precepts ; but we can easily see that it
is based on all the conditions we have

already discussed.   Some people attain it
through sympathy ; others through natural
intelligence ; others through a calm temper;
others again by observing closely the
mistakes of their neighbours.   As its
name implies, it is a sensitive touch in
social matters, which feels small changes
of temperature, and so guesses at changes
of temper ; which sees the passing cloud
on the expression of one face, or the
eagerness of another that desires to bring
out something personal for others to
enjoy.   This quality of tact is of course
applicable far beyond mere actual conversation.   In nothing is it more useful
than in preparing the right conditions
for a pleasant society, in choosing the
people who will be in mutual sympathy,
in thinking over pleasant subjects of talk
and suggesting them, in seeing that all
disturbing conditions are kept out, and
that the members who are to converse
may be secured from those small incon-

veniences which damage society so vastly
out of proportion to their intrinsic importance.

§ 25. This social skill is generally supposed to be congenital, especially in some
women, and no one thinks of laying down
rules for it, as its application is so constant, various, and often sudden.   Yet it
is certain that any one may improve himself by reflection on the matter, and so
avoid those shocking mistakes which arise
from social stupidity.   Thus, in the company of a woman who is a man's third
wife, most people will instinctively avoid
jokes about Blue Beard, or anecdotes of
comparison between a man's several wives,
of which so many are current in Ireland.
But quite apart from instinct, an experienced man who is going to tell a story
which may have too much point for some of
those present, will look round and consider
each member of the party, and if there be a
single stranger there whose views are not

familiar to him, he will forego the pleasure
of telling the story rather than make the
social mistake of hurting even one of the
guests.   On the other hand, this very
example shows how a single stranger
may spoil a whole conversation by in-
ducing caution in the speakers and im-
posing upon them such reserve as is in-
consistent with a perfectly easy flow of
talk.

Another evidence of tact is the perception that a topic has been sufficiently
discussed, and is on the point of becoming
tedious.   There is nothing in which elderly
people more frequently transgress, for even
those once gay and brilliant are almost
certain to become prosy with age, and to
dwell upon their favourite topics as if this
preference were shared by all society.   But
even the young are here also upon their
trial, and show their tact by refraining from
too many questions or too much argument
upon any single subject, which may be

tedious to others.[1] The ideal host and
hostess make it their first duty to watch
this human weakness, and to lead away the
conversation when it threatens to stay in
the same groove. It is better to do this
bluntly and confessedly than to refrain from
doing it. But the quality of tact, as it
quickly perceives the growing mischief, is
also quick of resource in devising such in-
terruptions as may seem natural or unavoid-
able, so as to beguile the company into new
paths, and even make the too persistent
members lay aside their threadbare discussion without regret.

[1] Even too careful an attention to grammar, and the
careful rounding of periods in easy intercourse, are apt
to be tedious. The instant the company has grasped his
idea, a good talker passes to something else without regard
to the form of his sentence.

CONDITIONS TOO GENERAL—MORAL
WORTH AND TRUTHFULNESS

§ 26. All the faculties hitherto enumerated are among those which are capable of
improvement by conscious training.   Yet
I have over and over again admitted that
nature — probably meaning by nature
heredity—has endowed some people with
gifts which others must strive to attain
by exercise. But I have hitherto excluded
such conditions as are either too wide
to be called conditions of conversation, or
too special ever to be attained without
great and peculiar natural gifts.

Of the first kind are general moral
worth and truthfulness, which afford the
proper ground for respect, and which
therefore give weight and importance to
anything the speaker says. In cases of
moral doubt, in cases of disputed fact, the
authority of such a person is a welcome

haven of rest for those that distrust other
evidence, and like a great authority in a
science expounding the principles of that
science, so a man or woman of high character may be of much service in conversation. But of course it would be ridiculous
to recommend the cultivation of this lofty
character for the sake of conversation. It
is perhaps more practical to observe that
an over-seriousness in morals may be detrimental to the ease and grace, above all to
the playfulness, of talk. Let me not be
misunderstood in this matter.[1] There is
no more valuable and useful check on the
degenerating of talk into ribaldry, pro-
fanity, or indecency, than the presence
of a mind of solid moral worth, which will
not tolerate such licence. There are companies, especially of young men, where such
things are taken for wit, and which thus

---

[1] In spite of this caution, I have been both misunderstood and misquoted, as I have shown in the new Preface
to this edition.

G

show a degradation of the conception of talk that would very soon render conversation intolerable to any intelligent man, not only from its coarseness but from its dulness. No man, no society, can be called witty, which has not far better credentials than that. Every company of men ought to import two or three grave and reverend people into their circle for the purpose of checking such ruinous excesses, if there be any probability that the conversation may stray into this slough of mire.

§ 27. But on the other hand, there is such a thing—Aristotle saw it long ago—as being over-scrupulous in truthfulness, when we are indulging in the relaxation of easy conversation. Even a consummate liar, though generally vulgar, and therefore offensive, will contribute more pleasantly to a conversation than the scrupulously truthful man, who weighs every statement, questions every fact, and corrects every

inaccuracy.[1] In the presence of such a
social scourge I have heard a witty talker
pronounce it the golden rule of conversation to *know nothing accurately.* Far more
important is it, in my mind, to *demand* no
accuracy. There is no greater or more
common blunder in society than to express disbelief or scepticism in a story told
for the amusement of the company. The object of the speaker is not to instruct, but
to divert, and to ask him : Is that really
true ? or to exclaim : Really that is too
much to expect us to believe ! shows that
the objector is a blockhead unfit for any
amusing conversation. The only social

---

[1] The teller of such stories should be justly ranked with
the novelist and the playwright, who compose fictions,
generally based on facts, for the entertainment of the
public. To censure a story for being false is almost as
foolish as to censure a novel for being fictitious. Many
tellers of good stories make themselves story-tellers by
alleging that they were themselves present when the thing
happened, or that they knew the actors. In this case
society resents perhaps the lie, certainly the audacity, of
the assertion.

treatment of such a story, if it be really beyond the bounds of reasonable belief, is either to receive with severe silence, or to out-do it with another still more extravagant, and so to bring back the company with laughter, and by excess of exaggeration to a soberer vein. The seriousness of the blunder just noted is not felt till we have learned that there is a vast number of real facts in nature so strange at first hearing that they excite active scepticism, and that you may lay a wager with any one to pass them off as lies. In fact, any society only familiar with one class of natural facts, can be furnished with facts from another sphere in nature which the majority will disbelieve.[1]

---

[1] For example, to men of town life, or of mere books, it will seem incredible that a fish should shoot flies with a drop of water, or that an otter should take a single bite out of a salmon and leave the rest, or that a woodcock should carry its young about in three different ways, all of which facts in natural history I have myself heard told to intelligent pedants, and set down by them as impudent inventions.

The point of importance in the present connection is, that if a man is reporting what he knows to be true and finds himself disbelieved, he will certainly either feel deeply hurt, or will conceive such contempt for the ignorance and bad manners of his hearers that he will make no further effort to help the conversation.

The outcome, therefore, of what has here been said about high moral worth and extreme truthfulness is, that these virtues, though lending the speaker dignity, may come to tyrannise over the lighter social graces. The great and good man must unbend ; he must acquiesce in being amused ; he must even connive at inaccuracies, and smile at what he considers inventions ; he must for the nonce regard recreation as his direct object if he is to be an active member in a pleasant company.

CONDITIONS TOO SPECIAL—WIT AND
HUMOUR

§ 28. There may have been times and
nations where conversation was regarded
as so serious and important an engine of
education, that sound argument, brilliant
illustration, and ample information, took
the highest place as qualities of talk.
Perhaps they do in some cases now, as,
for example, everybody who knows him
will concede to Mr. Gladstone the palm
as a very charming man in society by
reason of these qualities.   But among
hard-working and somewhat fatigued
people, who have been pursuing information of various kinds in all their working hours, conversation must be of the
nature of relaxation ; it must be amusing
first, instructive afterwards, and so it is
that nowadays no qualities, however
valuable, rank so high in popular esti-

mation for social purposes, as wit and
humour.

I will not ascend to a philosophical
analysis of these terms, or attempt to
answer the obscure and different question : What is it that makes us laugh,
and why we seem to have in this
somewhat trivial point a special feature
distinguishing us from all the lower animals ? They may have the faculty of
reason ; they seem entirely devoid of the
faculty of ridicule. Nay, even in the
scale of civilisation, it is remarkable that
the savage and the ignorant laugh less
and understand less of this great fund of
enjoyment than civilised people. There
are also, of course, national differences.
The English boor seldom laughs, and
then at very coarse fun ; the Italian or
the Irishman often, and very innocently ;
the modern Greek, though highly intelligent and keen, very seldom, apparently
from want of taste for the ridiculous.

As regards the distinction between wit
and humour, all I need here insist upon
is that the former consists in quick flashes,
in prompt repartee, in quaint comparison ;
while the latter is sustained ; it is a comic
way of looking at serious things, a flavour-
ing of narrative, a perception of the ludi-
crous vein in human life and character.
Both these are now esteemed very highly,
perhaps beyond their value, in society, but
they are so specially natural gifts, and
are so impossible to attain by practice,
that they cannot be required as conditions
to which every talker must conform ; they
can only be described, and their force or
weakness illustrated.

§ 29. There is nothing that requires to
appear spontaneous more stringently than
either of these qualities, and yet we read
of great wits, like Sheridan, who carefully
prepared their sallies, and even suborned
some one to lead up to them. The effect
of knowing this is to detract greatly from

the enjoyment of the company, and still
more from the reputation of the speaker.
Most of us would say, that however brilliant in writing comedies, Sheridan must
have been distinctly wanting in that
gift of spontaneous and ready wit which
flashes out at the least provocation, and
is mere intellectual playfulness, like the
playfulness of a young and happy animal.

So strongly do we feel this in Irish
society, where wit is less uncommon than
elsewhere, and where it is no less highly
prized, that a kind of social religion warns
us not to study it beforehand, and any one
suspected of coming out with prepared
smart things is received by the company
with ridicule.   Yet for all that, it cannot
possibly be denied that as most of the
brilliant things which a man uses in any
conversation must be at second hand—
to invent such things one after another
at the moment being beyond the power
of human genius—they must depend

upon a good memory, and this may best
be aided by having things written down,
which would else escape and be lost.

We should therefore conclude that
every man who goes into society, and has
an inclination for that kind of conversation, ought to keep some record of the
happy trifles he hears upon various occasions. But it seems, at least in Ireland,
as if the repugnance to doing this
amounted to a conclusive argument
against it. It is assumed that as surely
as a man has such a store, which he looks
up beforehand, so surely will he force the
conversation towards his points, or bring
them in when irrelevant ; and an irrelevant joke is hardly a real joke. I have
known, indeed, of a college Don having a
note-book of wit in his pocket, and peep-
ing at it under the table to refresh his
memory. This was regarded as far the
best joke about him, and the laughter
before he spoke was always greater than

when he had sped his shaft. In actual
society it has never occurred to me to
meet any one who has sustained a reputation for wit in this way. We think that
if the suggestion of the current conversation is not strong enough to bring up a
smart point naturally, and without effort,
it is better that it should be forgotten or
unsaid. Let me add the significant fact,
that in spite of endless attempts, no
printed collection of jokes has ever attained even a decent position in literature.[1]

So much for wit ; the case of humour
is slightly different.

HUMOUR

§ 30. If wit be the quick flash, the
electric spark, the play of summer light-
ning which warms the colour of con-

---

[1] I believe I should mention Dean Ramsay's well-
known book as an exception.

versation, humour is the sustained side
of the ridiculous, the comic way of looking at things and people, which may be
manifested either in comment upon the
statements made by others or in narrating one's own experiences.   Of course
in receiving and commenting upon what
is being said, no preparation is possible.
It depends altogether upon a mental attitude, which looks out with a smile upon
the world, and exposes the ridiculous side
of human life not more by irony of comment than by mock approval of social
vices, mock indignation at social virtues,
seriousness when false comedy is being
produced, raillery when false tragedy is
being paraded with insincerity or empty
bombast.   In these and a hundred other
ways humour receives and criticises what
other people say in a company ; and if
it be coupled *with kindliness of heart and
with tact,* may be regarded as the very
highest of conversational virtues.

Analogous to this is the display of
humour, not in receiving but in producing
ideas in company. The humorist is the
only good and effective story-teller ; for if
he is to monopolise a conversation, and
require others to listen to him, it must be
by presenting human life under a fresh
and piquant aspect—in fact, as a little
comedy. Thus the lifelike portrayal of
any kind of foible—pomposity, obsequiousness, conceit, hypocrisy, nay even of
provincial accent or ungrammatical language—ensures a pleased and therefore
agreeable audience, and opens the way for
easy and sympathetic intercourse. It is
perhaps not too much to say that in any
society where conventionality becomes a
threatening power, humour is our great
safeguard from this kind of vulgarity. Let
me point as an illustration of this to the
social sketches in *Punch*, which for years
back have been the truest mirror of the
vulgarities of English society. The humor-

ous exhibition of these foibles is the most effective way we know of bringing them before the public mind, and of warning people that here is a judge whose censure is really to be feared.   We may also learn from the success of this extraordinary paper how much more valuable and more respected prepared humour is than prepared wit.   The jokes in the text pass by unheeded, while the sketches of character are thought deserving of a permanent place in our literature.

§ 31. I need hardly add that the abuse of these great natural gifts is not only possible, but frequent, and in both it arises from the same mental defects — conceit and selfishness.   A man who can say a good thing or make a person appear ridiculous may be so proud of his power that he exercises it at the cost of good taste and even of real humanity.   The great wit is often cruel, and even glories in wounding to the quick the sensibilities of others.   If

he can carry some of the company with
him he has a wicked enjoyment in making one of the rest a butt or target for
his shafts, and so destroying all whole-
some conversation.   He may leave in the
minds of his society an admiration of his
talent, but often a serious dislike of his
character.   With such feelings abroad he
will injure conversation far more than he
promotes it.   People may consent to go
into his company to hear him talk, but
will avoid talking in his presence.

The excesses of the humorist are perhaps rather those of a complacent selfishness, which does not hesitate to monopolise
the company with long stories in which all
do not feel an interest.   But humour is its
own antidote ; and if a man have the true
vein in him he will also have the tact to
feel when he is tedious, and when his fun
is out of harmony with his hearers.   For
these reasons this quality is not only a
higher but a safer gift than wit for the

purposes of conversation ; the pity of it is
that so few possess it, and that there is
hardly any use in trying to attain it by
education.   No doubt the constant society
of an elder or superior who looks at things
in this way may stimulate it in the young ;
but there is the danger of making them
sarcastic and satirical, which are grave
faults, and which are the distortion of
humour to ill-natured and unsocial purposes, so that even in this view of the
matter education in humour may turn out
a very mischievous failure.

On the whole, we must set ourselves
to carry on society and to make good
conversation without any large help from
these brilliant but dangerous gifts.   Occasional flashes will occur to ordinary people,
and sometimes the very circumstances
themselves will create a situation so
comical that it requires no genius to
bring it home to the company.   But, beyond the considerations above indicated,

we cannot bring it into any systematic
doctrine of social intercourse.

OBJECTIVE CONDITIONS. THE COMPANY
—ITS NUMBER

§ 32. We have now exhausted all the
conditions which lie in the speaker,
which must be brought by him into a
society as the subjective conditions òf
good conversation. Let us turn to the
company, regarded as the object with
which he is to deal, and see what an
analysis of its varieties may teach us in
the way of practical direction.

The very first and most obvious division
is that of quantity. You may be required
to converse either with one person, with
a few, or with many. And though no
agreeable person may take the trouble
to think about it, he nevertheless makes
considerable modifications in his talk
according to these circumstances. Thus

a colloquy with a single person, which is the easiest form, for it is usually with some one who is not a stranger, and it allows far more personality, will best consist in a direct interchange of serious opinion, in which each seeks to make the other speak out in confidence his inmost character. The better talker will turn the conversation upon the other's life, inquire into his or her history, so far as that can be done with good taste and without impertinence, and so encourage him (or her) to give personal recollections or confessions, which are to the teller of them generally of the deepest interest. But you will not elicit these without some frankness on your own part, sometimes without volunteering some 'confidence' which may induce the other to open the flood-gates of his inner life. When this is once attained there must ensue good conversation ; for to have a volume of human character laid open before you, and to turn over its pages

at leisure, is one of the highest and most
intense recreations known to an intelligent
mind. Such confessions will hardly ever
be made to more than one person at a
time, and a sympathetic freedom in encouraging the timid by giving parallel experiences in your own life will often make a
silent and reserved person agreeable who
could never be persuaded to speak out in
a larger company.

As our manners and customs determine
these things, it is not usual to have a long
tête-à-tête with another person of the same
sex without choosing your companion and
seeking out the opportunity ; but, on the
contrary, two people of different sexes are
often brought together and ordered (so to
speak) to converse, for no other reason
than the command of society. Thus a
young man is introduced to a partner at a
ball, or a man of soberer age is directed
to take a lady down to dinner. Here,
though the company is large, the conver-

sation is really of the kind before us—
a dialogue between two persons only, of
different sexes, and often comparative
strangers.   There is no case more frequent
where conversation is imperative, and where
failures are common and conspicuous.   It
is commonplace enough to begin with
truisms about the weather—an excusable
exordium ; it is far worse and almost dis-
graceful to end with them, and positively
many people get no further.   And yet
this failure is not from mere emptiness of
mind.   These very same people, young
and old, could be brought into circumstances where almost any of them would be
interesting—not a few of them eloquent.

I have spent an evening shut up with
a very unpromising commercial traveller
in a remote country inn, and yet by trying
honestly to find out what he knew and
liked, succeeded in drawing from him a
most interesting account of his experiences, first in tea-tasting, then in tea-

selling to the Irish peasants in the remote
glens of Donegal. What he told me
was quite worthy to make an article in a
good magazine. Yet a more unpromising
subject for a long dialogue could hardly
be found. He and I had apparently not
a single interest in common. But when
the right vein was touched one had to
supply nothing but assent, or an occasional question ; the man flowed on
with an almost natural eloquence. People
said that others had found him morose
and unapproachable. It was certainly
their fault. This case is cited as an instance that almost anybody can be made
to talk, unless he has determined positively
that he will not do so, and is moreover a
very obstinate person.

§ 33. In the cases with which we started
no such obstinacy exists ; the people are
really ready to talk, but don't know how.
The beginning is evidently the difficulty ;
and surely here, if anywhere, people who

have no natural facility should think out
some way of opening the conversation,
just as chessplayers have agreed on several
formal openings in their game. Nothing
is easier than to do this, and to do it in
such a general manner as will not be
ridiculous. It must always be remembered
that the most domestic men and women
are often the most difficult to rouse into
conversation. Their very virtues in home
life have absorbed their interests in outer
things, and the best of mothers have sometimes forgotten to talk about anything
except the education of their children.
But it is always better worth probing a
sound nature than tolerating the ready
chatter of idleness. For this reason, some
serious topic ought to be the best, even
for talking with a stranger, since our
conversation errs more frequently through
frivolity than through gravity.

But it is not the object of this book to
be a practical guide, with special directions.

They are only useful when framed by each man and woman for their own private use, and any stock proceeding becomes a mere commonplace, and as such contemptible. Yet no intelligent person who thinks over it can fail to make out some general lines to be followed on such occasions, and so thousands of men and women will save themselves from the punishment of a dull and tedious evening beside a person whom they might easily find lively and agreeable.

As there are some people who require to be encouraged by finding out their daily interests, and inquiring into them, so there are others who are only to be excited by the stimulus of opposition, by suggesting some opinion adverse to what they believe or advocate, and so tempting them to a friendly controversy. If people enter such a controversy with perfectly good temper, with a desire to be convinced by good arguments, and no further interest than to bring out the latent fire in the rest, it may produce a very good conversation. But the moment the points of difference become too strongly accentuated, the moment there arises that dissatisfaction which is so common in people who are losing ground, or who feel they are making no impression, it is time to turn the stream into another channel, in which at least partial agreement can fairly be anticipated.

Talking with a Few

§ 34. These last remarks are very applicable to the case next before us, when conversation is among a few—say from four to eight people—a form of society the best and most suitable for talk, but which is now rather the exception, from the common habit of crowding our rooms or our tables, and getting rid of social obligations as if they were commercial debts. Indeed many of our young people have so seldom heard a general conversation that they grow up in the belief that their only duty in society will be to talk to one man or woman at a time. So serious are the results of the fashion of large dinner-parties. For really good society no dinner-table should be too large to exclude general conversation, and no couples should sit together who are likely to lapse into private discourse.

It is generally thought the fault of the host or hostess if such an evening turns out a failure ;[1] and indeed it is possible to bring one incongruous person into a small company, who will so chill or annoy the rest that conversation languishes. But this

---

[1] It is right to add that there are hosts and hostesses so anxious for the good entertainment of their friends that this preoccupation spoils their own enjoyment, and so far defeats the very object they have in view. But people so truly desirous of giving pleasure can hardly avoid being pleasant in a better sense than those who do not feel their responsibilities so acutely.

case is rare, and the fault usually lies with
the company, none of whom take the
trouble to tide over any difficulty, or seek
to draw out from those present what they
like or want to say.   I am now looking
at the thing from the point of view of
the man or woman who comes in as a
guest, and whose duty it is to make the
evening, or the period of time during
which the company is assembled, pass in
a pleasant way.   Perhaps it is the easiest
course to consider the usual form in
modern society, that of the small dinner-
party, and then apply what is to be said
upon it to analogous cases.

In the very forefront there stares us in
the face that very awkward period which
even the gentle Menander notes as the
worst possible for conversation, the short
time during which people are assembling,
and waiting for the announcement of
dinner.   If the witty man were not
usually a selfish person, who will not

exhibit his talent without the reward of
full and leisurely appreciation, this is
the real moment to show his powers.
A brilliant thing said at the very
start, which sets people laughing, and
makes them forget that they are waiting,
may alter the whole complexion of the
party, may make the silent and distant people feel themselves drawn into
the sympathy of common merriment, and
thaw the iciness which so often fetters
Anglo-Saxon society.   But as this faculty
is not given to many, so the average man
may content himself with having something ready to tell, and this, if possible, in
answer to the usual question expressed or
implied : Is there any news this after-
noon ?   There are few days that the daily
papers will not afford to the intelligent
critic something ridiculous either in style
or matter which has escaped the ordinary
public ; some local event, nay, even some
local tragedy, may suggest a topic not

worth more than a few moments of attention, which will secure the interest of
minds vacant, and perhaps more hungry
to be fed than their bodies.   Here then,
if anywhere in the whole range of conversation, the man and woman who desire
to be agreeable may venture to think
beforehand, and bring with them something ready, merely as the starting-point
to make the evening run smoothly.

§ 35. When the company has settled
down to dinner, the first danger impend-
ing is the breaking into couples, which
will certainly happen unless some one
opposite is addressed or some question
asked which may evoke answers from various people.   Above all, however, the particular guest of the night, or the person
best known as a wit or story-teller, is *not*
to be pressed or challenged at the outset
—a sort of vulgarity which makes him
either shy or angry at being so manifestly
exploité by the company, so that he is

likely either to turn silent or say some ill-humoured things.

The resource least utilised by women to help them in making such a small company agreeable, is an acquaintance with politics.[1] A vast number of clever and well-read women exclude themselves from a large part of the serious talk of men by neglecting this engrossing and ever-fruitful topic of conversation. Literature of course, is a still more various and interesting subject ; but here perhaps the defect lies with men, who are so devoted to practical life that they lose their taste for general reading. Except for politics, the daily papers seldom afford any serious literary food fit for good conversation.

The topic which ought to be common to both and always interesting, is the discussion of human character and human motives. If the novel be so popular a form of literature, how can the novel in

[1] On this point see the Preface to this edition.

real life fail to interest an intelligent company? People of serious temper and
philosophic habit will be able to confine
themselves to large ethical views, and
the general dealings of men ; but to
average people, both men and women,
and perhaps most of all to busy men,
who desire to find in society relaxation
from their toil, that lighter and more personal kind of criticism on human affairs
will prevail which is known as *gossip*.

§ 36. This may, therefore, be the suitable moment to consider the place of
gossip in the theory of conversation ; for
though gossip is not only possible but
usual in the private discourse of two
people, and possible too in a large society,
its real home and natural exercising ground
is the society of a few people intimate with
the same surroundings.

It is usual for all people, especially
those who most indulge in it, to censure
gossip as a crime, as a violation of the

Ninth Commandment, as a proof of idleness and vain curiosity, as a frivolous
waste of the time given us for mental
improvement.   Yet the censure is seldom
serious.   These people cannot but feel
obscurely what they are either afraid to
speak out or have not duly considered,
that the ordinary object of conversation is
neither instruction nor moral improvement, but *recreation*.   It is of course highly
desirable that all our amusements should
be both intellectually and morally profitable, and we may look back with
special satisfaction upon any conversation which included these higher advantages.   But the ordinary and direct object
is recreation, mental relaxation, happy
idleness; and from this point of view
it is impossible for any honest theory of
conversation to ignore or depreciate gossip,
which is perhaps the main factor in agreeable talk throughout society.

The most harmless form is the repeating of small details about personages great either in position or intellect, which give their empty names a personal colour, and so bring them nearer and more clearly into view.   The man who has just come from the society of kings and queens, or great generals, or politicians, or literary men whose names are exceptionally prominent at the time, can generally furnish some personal details by which people imagine they can explain to themselves great and unexpected results.   Who has not heard with interest such anecdotes about Mr. Gladstone, or Prince Bismarck, or Victor-Emmanuel ?   And what book has ever acquired more deserved and lasting reputation than Boswell's *Life of Johnson ?*

The latest development of the literary side of gossip is to be seen in what are called the ' society papers,' which owe their circulation to their usefulness in furnishing topics for this kind of conversation.[1] All the funny sketches of life and character which have made *Punch* so admirable a mirror of society for the last fifty years, are of the character of gossip, subtracting the mischievous element of personality ; and though most people will think this latter an essential feature in our meaning when we talk of gossip, it is not so ; it is merely the trivial and passing, the unproven and suspected, which constitutes gossip, for it is quite possible to bring any story under the notion while suppressing the names of the actors.

Next to the retailing of small personal points about great people comes the narrating of deeper interests belonging to small people, especially the affairs of the heart, which we pursue so assiduously even in feigned characters. But here it is that all the foibles of our neighbours

---

[1] I only speak of the *fact* that they are useful in supplying a want. Whether they are or are not corrupting the public mind is another and a very serious question.

I

come under survey, and that a great deal
of calumny and slander may be launched
upon the world by mere shrug and in-
nuendo. The reader will remember with
what effect this mischievous side of gossip
is brought out in Sheridan's *School for
Scandal.*

§ 37. It is idle to deny that there is
no kind of conversation more fascinating
than this, but its immorality may easily
become such as to shock honest minds,
and the person who indulges in it freely at
the expense of others, will probably have
to pay the cost himself in the long
run ; for those who hear him will fear
him, and will retire into themselves in his
presence. On the other hand, nothing is
more honourable than to stand forth as
the defender or the palliator of the faults
imputed to others, and nothing is easier
than to expand such a defence into
general considerations as to the purity
of human motives, which will raise the

conversation from its unwholesome ground
into the upper air.

If the company be fit for it, no general
rule is more valuable than that of turning
the conversation away from people and
fixing it on things ; but, alas ! how many
there are who only take interest in people,
and in the weakest and most trivial
aspects of people !   Few things are more
essential and more neglected in the education of children than to habituate them
to talk about things, and not people ; yet,
what use is there in urging these more
special rules, when the very idea of teaching them to converse at all is foreign to
the minds of most parents and of all
educators ?   Let me illustrate this by one
grotesque fact.

It will be conceded that one thing absolutely essential to the education of a
lady is that she should talk agreeably at
meals.   It is the natural meeting time,
not only of the household, but of friends,

and conversation is then as essential as
food.   Yet, what is the habit of many of
our schools ?   They either enforce silence
at this period, or they compel the wretched
pupils to speak in a foreign language, in
which they can only labour out spasmodic
commonplaces, without any interchange
or play of thought.   Consequently many
of our girls drift into the habit of regarding meal-times as the precise occasion
when conversation is impossible.   How far
this mis-education, during some of the
most critical years of their lives, affects
them permanently it is not easy to over-
estimate.   If parents were decently intelligent in this matter they should ascer-
tain clearly the practice of a school, and
the schoolmaster or schoolmistress who is
obtuse or mischievous enough to practise
this absurdity should at once lose every
pupil.

The only excuse I can find for this
widespread outrage upon the social rights

of the young, is the old tradition of uni-
versities, still pursued in convent schools
and Roman Catholic seminaries, that a
portion of Scripture, or of some edifying
book, should be read out during meals,
so that the pupils may take in spiritual
food along with their dinners, and avoid
the crime of light and trivial conversation.
A clever Jesuit educator whom I knew,
went so far within the letter of the law as
to substitute the *Saturday Review* for the
usual work of edification, the *Lives of the
Saints!* This worthy man did what was
possible under a system devised to bring
up young people in silence and in fear,
not in free and friendly intercourse with
their instructors. But why should we,
with our spiritual liberty, retain these mischievous and antiquated shackles?

With Many

§ 38. Conversation with a crowd, or
even with a large number of people, is
almost a contradiction in terms. How
can there be interchange of thought or
repartee where so many clashing fancies
make confusion rather than harmony?
In ordinary society, therefore, it is the
obvious solution to break up a large company into couples or small groups, and so
reduce this case to one of the preceding.
Two exceptional forms may be noted,
which come, perhaps, upon the verge of
conversation proper: the one where a good
story-teller, or person who has had some
wonderful experience, is ready to talk for
the benefit of the whole company, with
occasional support from questions put to
him by various people. But even in this
case the number must be limited, and
usually such a talker will seem to his

audience egotistical, for people who want to have their little private say, and tell their little modest story, feel ousted by the monopoly of the leading spirit.

Perhaps the pleasantest form into which to lead such a conversation is a sort of public dialogue, in which one or two querists will draw from the real object of attention his views, or 'question his statements in such a way as to provoke the exercise of his powers. This is the kind of conversation to be found in Plato's *Dialogues*, which are quite fitted for a large company, though but few speakers share in them. But I will not be bound to admire these immortal compositions as specimens of conversation. To the modern reader, they cease to be such as soon as they become serious, and I may even venture to say that in any modern society they would justly be voted tedious.

§ 39. The second case worth noticing here is when a leading person, king or

viceroy, or princess, or political magnate,
entertains a crowd of people mostly inferior in station, and has to perform the
duty of going through the rooms and
talking in succession to all sorts and conditions of men.   If on the one hand the
people addressed are sure to be flattered
by such attention, and are therefore re-
sponsive and anxious to be pleased, on
the other there is no social duty which
gives more scope for all the mental and
moral perfections already enumerated, and
therefore there is no more certain test of
conversational ability.   For here the talk
is not really with many at a time, nor
again is it the conversation with one
person, in which the main element is the
sustaining of interest for a considerable
time ; it is a series of brief successive
dialogues, in which the two great difficulties of conversation, the starting of it and
the breaking off, are perpetually recurring.
The speaker is even debarred from the

use of any fixed rule or method of overcoming these difficulties, for the people
addressed will be sure to compare notes,
and will reject as insincere any politenesses
which are administered according to a
formula, however graceful it may appear.

Here then, if anywhere, the art must
consist in concealing the art. But let none
imagine that art has no place here. A
sympathetic nature, which readily appre-
hends the interests of other minds, is not
more useful to the great man or woman
than a careful previous study of the company, who they are, what they have done,
what the distinction or the hobby of each
of them may be. Nothing is easier than
to acquire such information from the
retinue whose duty is to furnish it. A
great natural aptitude or a specially
trained memory is required to remember
the various scraps of information about
each, and to fit them to the proper names.
It is said that royal personages often in-

herit an exceptional power of remembering names and persons from the exercise of this faculty by a long line of successive ancestors. But the suggestion of an equerry or a lord-in-waiting is in such cases the usual and more obvious cause of this apparent genius, which the flattery of courtiers exaggerates with shameless effrontery.

However this may be, the knowledge, inspired or acquired, of the name and circumstances of an inferior is the great key to smoothing over the difficulty of beginning a conversation, for any personal question will be taken as a compliment, and evidence of a friendly interest on the part of the prince. The breaking off with ease and grace is more difficult, for I do not count the formal bow of dismissal or the prearranged interruption by a new presentation as more than awkward subterfuges. Some form of expressing regret that the moment does not admit of fuller

discussion of the subject already com-
menced, and a hope to resume it, is of
course an obvious and polite way of clos-
ing the interview, or a question as to some
one else who must receive attention, or a
complaint that duty must oust pleasure—
there are myriad possibilities, as may be
seen from the conversation of the few
great ladies in England who have the gift
or have attained the art. I mention ladïes,
because the traditional bluntness and
simplicity inherited, respected, assumed,
affected, by most Englishmen makes them
very averse to this social grace. It is no
accident that those of our great houses
who have adopted public life after a considerable experience of French manners,
and with a ready knowledge of the French
language, are the most brilliant exceptions.
Perhaps, too, Irish vivacity has in most
of these cases added life and brightness
to their talk. But, as a rule, it is to
women that we look for this talent, and to

older French society for the best examples
of it.   One often hears it said that since
Lady Waldegrave's death no one in London knows how to have a *salon*.   This,
though it is false, is the popular recogni-
tion of that social excellence in conversing
with many, to which I have devoted the
last few pages.

The Quality of the Company

§ 40. Hitherto we have regarded the
company merely from the point of quantity, and considered them as so many
units, grouped in larger and smaller
masses.   We shall now adopt a totally different principle, and regard their quality in
relation to the speaker.   It is obvious that
for our purpose this element must receive
careful consideration.

I remember years ago occupying myself
in constructing from the epitaphs in a
country church the genealogy of the great

squire who owned the parish.   Among the
stereotyped and hardly varied eulogies of
his ancestors one stood out as peculiar and
original.   It was said of this magnate,
who died about the year 1830, that to
express his virtues among those that knew
him would be impertinent, 'but to strangers
and to posterity let this monument declare,
that in him were combined *the generous
Patron, the affable Superior, the polished
Equal,* the uncompromising Patriot, and the
Honest Man.'   The sequel was commonplace.   Nor is the social description complete, for the dignity of the subject would
not allow the epitaphist to suggest the
virtues of his hero in the guise of an inferior.   *The supple courtier* would, from
what I have heard about him, have been
the truest addition to the picture.   But
what interests us here is not only the
importance given to social talents over
morals and religion,—a truly Irish feature,
—but the accurate perception the writer

had of the various talents required according to the quality of the people around us.

If he had thought more upon the subject, or if he had been allowed to give us the results of his thinking, he might have told us that the secret in all cases, and the *sine qua non* of good conversation, is to establish equality, at least momentary, if you like fictitious, but at all costs *equality*, among the members of the company who make up the party. The man who keeps asserting his superiority, or confessing his inferiority, is never agreeable. Nay even, if the superiority is very marked, as in the case of royal persons, it is almost impossible to converse with them in the better sense, and one of the most melancholy penalties of this kind of greatness is, that except within the narrow circle of their families and equals they can never enjoy the fresh breeze of unconstrained society. Any truth they can learn from their surroundings is confined to the very

poor category of pleasant truths. All
vigorous intellectual buffeting, all whole-
some contradiction which would open their
minds, is carefully avoided by courtiers,
and yet it is the assertion of this very
equality which is the backbone of conversation. It requires peculiar earnestness
and honesty on the part of a prince to
break through this crust of assentation,
and discover the real opinions of the men
around him ; nor can he incur any bitterer
loss than the removal of those rare
advisers, who have the gift of combin-
ing real liberty with formal obsequiousness,
and without violating the etiquette of the
court, can assume the character of independent critics and just advisers.

But this little book is not meant for the
advice or criticism of kings, who by their
position are almost completely excluded
from conversation. The question before
us is how far we ordinary people modify
the tone of our talk according as our com-

pany consists of people socially or intellectually above us, of our equals, or lastly,
of our inferiors.   It is evident that in
the first and last cases there is difficulty ;
the second is the normal atmosphere of
conversation.

TALKING WITH SUPERIORS

§ 41. In conversing with superiors, we
must broadly distinguish the socially from
the intellectually superior.   For the art of
producing agreeable talk in the former
case differs widely from the art of doing
so in the latter.   Perhaps the matter may
be expressed tersely, if not quite accurately, by saying that the necessary
equality between the members of the
company is attained in the former instance
by the good talker raising himself to the
level of his superior, in the latter by
bringing down his superior to his own
level.   A word of explanation is here

necessary. The man or woman that succeeds among social superiors is not the
timid or modest person, afraid to contradict, and ever ready to assent to what is
said, but rather the free and independent
intellect that suggests subjects, makes bold
criticisms, and in fact introduces a bright
and free tone into a company which is
perhaps somewhat dull from its grandeur
or even its extreme respectability. It is
a case of the socially superior acknow-
ledging another kind of superiority, which
redresses the balance. We need hardly
add that the greatest stress must here
be placed on tact, for to presume on either
kind of superiority will cause offence, and
so spoil every attempt at breaking the
bonds set around us by the grades of the
social hierarchy.

If, on the contrary, we meet a man of
acknowledged mental superiority, whether
generally or in his special department, it
is our social duty by intelligent question-

ing, by an anxiety to learn from him, to force him to condescend to our ignorance, or join in our fun, till his broader sympathies are awakened, and he plays with us as if we were children. Indeed this very metaphor points out one of the very remarkable instances of social equality asserted by an inferior—I mean the outspoken freedom of the child—which possesses a peculiar charm, and often thaws the dignity or dissipates the reserve of the great man and woman whose superiority is a perpetual obstacle to them in ordinary society.

I may here dwell a moment upon conscious superiority and its companion, that conscious inferiority, which is the great social barrier to conversation, and which in most cases actually prohibits all intercourse. In other European countries the separation of *noblesse* and *bourgeoisie* is carried so far as wellnigh to annihilate all free and intellectual society of the better kind. The intellectually-educated classes are so thoroughly excluded from social education in the urbanity and grace of noble society, that they sink into mere intellectual boors, while the aristocrats so seldom hear any intellectual discussion or take any interest in learning that their society becomes either vapidly trivial or professionally narrow. For these nobles have their professions like other people, especially the profession of arms.

The case is not so bad among us, where there are always great commoners, where eminent success in making money, or even in letters, brings men and women into the highest society, and where there are some of the greatest positions in the country from which our Peers are excluded. There is no doubt that an intellectual man, or a man of strong and recognised character, whatever his origin, can easily take a place in high society among us. But how many lesser people are there of ex-

cellent social gifts who assume most falsely
that they are not suited, and will not be
welcome, to the higher classes, and so
avoid both the pleasure and the profit to
be derived from a more refined, though not
more cultivated, stratum than their own !
I am here talking of really modest and
worthy people, not of those vain and vulgar persons who make it a boast—often a
very dishonest one—that they have spurned
associating with their superiors, from a profound contempt of what they call *toadyism*.

§ 42. This term, which expresses the
vicious relations of socially inferior and
superior, is used in very vague senses,
ranging from a just censure of meanness
in others to a mistaken assertion of inde-
pendence in ourselves. Nothing is more
inherent in all European society derived
from the feudal and ecclesiastical traditions
of the Middle Ages—probably in every
cultivated society—than to honour rank
and social dignity as such, apart from the

real worth of the person so distinguished.
This is the basis of that loyalty to sov-
rans which, even when irrational, does
not incur the imputation of toadyism.
People of independent rank and personal dignity even still accept and prize
semi-menial offices about a court, without losing either respect among ordinary
people or even self-respect.

There is then such a thing as respect for
rank as such, and a feeling of pride in the
contact with it, which is regarded as honourable.   When does the virtue of loyalty
pass into a vice ?   Clearly when the higher
and more important duties of life are
postponed to this love of outward dignity.
The man who neglects his equals for the
purpose of courting his superiors ; still
more, who confesses or asserts his inferiority when associating with them, and
who submits to rebuffs and indignities for
the sake of being thought their associate ;
above all, who condones in them vices

which he would not tolerate in an equal
—this man is justly liable to the charge,
which, however, only asserts the exaggeration of a tendency affecting almost all his
censors.

The usual thing, however, is to hear
people censured for the *fact* of associating
with those above them, as if this were
in itself a crime.   There is, too, not unfrequently an element of jealousy in our
criticism, and of secret regret that another
has attained certain advantages, or supposed advantages, to which we ourselves
feel an equal claim.   Yet one thing is
certain, that if the supposed toady ex-
hibited in the society which he courts
the qualities ascribed to him by his critics,
he would very soon lose his position
and miss the very object of his ambition.
The only cause of his popularity is the
very fact that his company feel him in
some respects their equal, possibly their
superior, and it is the secret of asserting

this equality with tact and courtesy which makes men and women popular among their superiors.

There is one point of view which gives a good talker a distinct advantage under these circumstances. The distinctness of his ordinary associates from those whom he occasionally meets makes his everyday experience different from theirs, so that things familiar to him and his everyday society are often interesting and novel to people of a different standing. He ought therefore to be able to bring new information to bear upon either class of society, so as to secure its interest with his store of fresh experiences.

WITH INFERIORS

§ 43. Let us now turn to the other side and consider the proper principles of conversation with inferiors. And here, too, it is more practical to take our stand-

point in the middle class of society, and
not among those who must habitually
talk to inferiors owing to their own
high condition. The same key un-
locks the secret of success. If it be
indispensable for good conversation to
make your superiors feel you for the
time their equal, so it is indispensable
that your inferiors should feel that they
too are upon a social level with you
during their talk. Of course, the first
thing is to banish all traces of *con-
descension*, that odious ape of humility
and urbanity, which is the loud expression of want of brains and want of tact,
for it emphasises the very differences
which conversation seeks to obliterate.
On the other hand, there is an extreme
of *familiarity* which shocks and alarms
the inferior, for he justly expects a sudden
revulsion from it, as we are told in Poly-
bius of the common people of Antioch,
into whose humble entertainments or

amusements Antiochus Epiphanes would come, and sit down to drink and joke with them. These vagaries on the part of their despotic sovran so frightened them that they would get up and run away. The just mean is to strike out a line of conversation, either of common interest, or in which the inferior is a specialist, and therefore your superior. He will then feel that he is speaking with authority, and the honest expression of your ignorance and your desire to learn will give him confidence to tell you freely what he knows.

§ 44. It is in the lower ranks of society that national differences become really great. The highly bred or highly cultivated people of any European nation have attained a certain unity of type, and are interested by the same sort of conversation ; it is very different with English, French, Italian, and German peasants. Nay, even within our islands, there is a

marked difference in the social abilities
of English, Scotch, and Irish peasants.
It is customary to set this down to race,
and be satisfied with some such vague
generality.   But I fancy the causes of these
social differences are rather recent than
primeval ; they do not depend directly
upon climate or atmosphere, and if I
may quote the opinion of a wise friend
on this large question, possibly one chief
cause of the talking or social ability of
some peasantries over others is the fact
that their proximate ancestors were a
bilingual people. Thus the great majority
of West Irish and North Scotch peasants
are descended from grandfathers whose
talk oscillated between Celtic and English,
and who were therefore constantly educated
in intelligence by the problem of *translat-
ing* ideas from one language into another,
not to mention the distinct inheritance
of the special ideas peculiar to each and
every language.   This is an education in

expression, in thinking, and therefore in conversation, wholly foreign to the English Midland boor, who has never heard more than two or three hundred words of a very rude provincial dialect of English, and therefore commands neither the words nor the ideas of the outlying provinces. A great part of the French peasantry are likewise proximately descended from bilingual ancestors, French being the old language of but a small part of their now recognised territory. Breton, Bearnais, Provencal, Walloon, are even still living languages in large parts of France (as was German up to 1871), and so the peasantry were under like favourable conditions.[1]

[1] The *Spectator*, in an able article on this point, argued that there was not sufficient evidence to prove this theory. Perhaps so. But some of the cases quoted against me were hardly in point. Thus the writer asked whether the Parisians were inferior in talking to the bilingual French in the country, as if the education of a great and gay city were not a disturbing element completely precluding all just comparison. For I compared the country man in England with the country people in France. It

But I must not diverge further from
the subject in hand. Thus much was
naturally suggested to me by the best
and most diverting conversation I know
with inferiors—that which sporting men
have with those whose livelihood has been
earned by studying the habits and ways
of fish and game. There are few men
who shoot, fish, or hunt in Ireland, who
do not know specimens of that remarkable though small class whose natural
ability, combined with long experience,
makes them masters of their craft, and
whose long association with their superiors
in matters of sport has given them perfect
ease and even charm of manners. Conversation with these people, which is
often prolonged through many hours, is

was also argued that English country women talk well
enough though they are not bilingual. If they do, we
should compare them with similar women in other
countries. I do not feel bound to the theory suggested
in the text, but should like to see it refuted by the
citation of really parallel cases on the other side.

not only very instructive—a secondary
matter to us now—but exceedingly amusing, from the perfect frankness as well as
tact with which they speak their mind to
the sporting friend, whom they regard
as their inferior or equal from a profes-
sional point of view. It is this perfect
liberty, this spiritual equality, often desig-
nated as the freemasonry of sport, from
which arises the charm of talking upon
subjects of common interest to one confessedly inferior in many respects. But
in one he is commonly your superior,
even apart from his sport. It has been
far more important to him all his life to
study and know the characters of his
employers than it has been for them to
study his, and so he is generally your
superior in perceiving what will please,
and what topics are to be selected or
avoided in conversation. Nothing has
struck me more in many such talks than
the acute estimate which these people

form of the strength and weakness of those who are their patrons.

These are illustrations of a general kind, to show how inferiority in social station may not imply inferiority for the purposes of conversation, so that we may even here attain that equality which I regard as essential for its success.

THE RELATIONS OF SEX AND AGE

§ 45. So far we have been considering the quality of the company as determined by social position, which, if not an absolutely artificial distinction, is at least frequently such, so that it may be even reversed by circumstances. There are great distinctions made by nature which are indelible, and which must therefore be reckoned with as permanent factors in our theory—I mean those of age and sex.

There are, properly speaking, three

grades of age worth considering—youth,
maturity, and old age ; but from our
point of view we are justified in regarding mature life as the normal state, and
shall therefore consider the duties of the
mature man and woman as they come in
contact with the extremes. It is not
worth while writing any advices for the
old, as they are beyond the age of improvement, though by no means always
stripped of their social qualities ; indeed,
the position of very old people, who have
maintained their faculties, is quite exceptional in modern society, and will require a few words of comment in the
present connection.

A collection of very old people is of
course hardly to be found ; so that the
practical case before us is the occurrence
of one, or at most two, very old people
in a company, and the consequent modifications in ordinary society likely to
make this element effective and agree-

able. It may almost be assumed that
however lively the old person is, he (or
she) will not be able to converse when
many people are talking in the room, and
to assert himself in even a small crowd.
There must be comparative silence while
he is speaking, and special attention should
be paid him.   Under these circumstancès
it almost follows as a matter of course
that he should be discreetly drawn out to
tell such experiences as are beyond the
memory of the rest, which from their
pictures of bygone manners or long dead
celebrities are very interesting, and ad-
mirably suited for the best social recreation.
The many *Recollections*, *Diaries*, *Autobiographies*, etc., now published from the
papers of the mere observers of their age,
such as Greville, and which are generally
too trivial and minute to make good
books, form the staple of excellent conversation when told by the very actor or
observer.   Of course there is a consider-

able chance of his becoming tedious ; it is
one of the most frequent defects of age ;
but if a man's hobby makes him tedious,
it may also make him very interesting ;
and the first and best receipt to make a
man agreeable is to make him talk about
what he likes best.

The most successful conversations with
old men are, however, not those with the
old *raconteur*, who is in the habit of narrating his experiences and expects to be
asked to do so, but with some modest
and apparently dull old person who is
successfully probed by intelligent and
sympathetic questions, till he is actually
reminded of long-forgotten scenes, which
have perhaps not been suggested to him
for years, and then he draws from his
memory, with the help of further questions,
some passage of life and adventure of the
highest interest. Many a time have I
seen an old person, at first regarded as an
obstacle, prove the highest advantage to

L

the conversation, and it is for this reason
that in a book of theory the reader should
be reminded that here is a valuable item
which is often heedlessly thrown away.
It is generally easy enough to gather from
the old gentleman (or lady) where he has
lived, what society he has frequented, and
what are his strongest impressions as to
the contrasts between his own early days
and ours.

There is allowed, moreover, in discussing the gossip and the scandal of a
bygone generation an amount of freedom
—I had almost said licence—which would
be intolerable as regards living society,
and a very old person may be allowed to
say things which younger people should
avoid.   I do not mention this as an
advantage in itself—far from it—but as
an additional possibility in making conversation lively, and in avoiding that stag-
nation in talk which, from our present point
of view, is the worst fault known to society,

It is also obvious that as old people
are unable to talk loudly and with vivacity,
the dialogue between two, or a couple of
listeners added to the questioner, will be
the most likely way to attain the end in
view.   To stop an old person who is
becoming tedious is probably the most
difficult of all social duties, and requires
the most delicate tact.   The respect due to
age takes from our hands those weapons
of sarcasm, banter, or even blunt interruption which are our natural defences against
obtrusive youth ; it is fortunate that the
theorist is not required to lay down
general directions which can deliver a
host or hostess in this grave and not
uncommon difficulty.   It is of course
useless to lecture old people, either - in
this book or elsewhere, on the dangers of
tediousness.

§ 46. I turn now to conversation with
people much younger that ourselves, not
of course with babies, or very young

children, the art of amusing whom can hardly be called the art of conversation. I mean rather such ordinary cases as going in to dinner with a person much younger than yourself, whose main interests must therefore be foreign to yours ; or else the entertaining of a party of young people who have met for purposes of sport, but are also to be regarded as guests at a table where conversation asserts its universal importance.

What modifications in our talk are here desirable ?

In the first place it is but natural for the older person to lead the discourse, and suggest the topics which will elicit sympathy from the young. And of course the easiest way to begin is to make people talk about themselves—this being a subject which interests most young people exceedingly. But it is by no means an universal rule. The life of the young, of schoolboys, and of young girls, is often very monotonous, and really affords no scope for conversation beyond the first ordinary inquiries into their tastes, habits, and what they read. If there be a strong taste for any special thing, such as music or cricket, the difficulty is easily overcome.

But if, as is too often the case, the youth has not thought seriously about anything, the elder must draw from his own stores, and tell experiences which will be new and interesting from their curiosity, such as the ways and habits of the lower animals which he may have observed, the manners of men, or of strange cities which he has visited, the feats he has seen performed. These things are seldom suitable for other kinds of society, when any display of experiences is offensive ; but in talking to young, fresh, and ingenuous people, the novelty of the information given them will generally obscure their critical or fault-finding sense, and even if they are very sceptical as to facts,—the young and inexperienced in our day are usually so,—they will fully appreciate the effort to make them feel happy.

§ 47. It is perhaps not till then that the talker will succeed in finding out some interesting nook in their short experience. They have been in accidental contact with some great or notorious person, and have seen him in his leisure moments ; they may have lived in a peculiar country, where either the sport or the natural features are very interesting, and upon which they can have the distinction of instructing older and wiser people.

I have met quiet country gentlemen who in their youth had seen active service in the army, and fought in remarkable campaigns, who never spoke of these things among their neighbours, so that when some intelligent stranger drew from them their experiences, it came like a revelation to those who for years had voted them stupid and dull members of a county society.

So important and so neglected is this social duty of probing for the strong point of others, which is naturally brought forward in connection with the effort to talk with the young and inexperienced, that I am disposed to lay this down as a practical rule: *if you find the company dull, blame yourself.* With more skill and more patience on your part it is almost certain you would have found it agreeable. If even two or three people in a company acted on this rule, how seldom would our social meetings prove a failure!

§ 48. We come now to a still more indelible contrast than that of age, and ask what effects, advantageous or otherwise, has the contrast of sex upon conversation? It is a problem very difficult indeed to solve, for while it is a great law of nature that the very instincts of each sex urge it to please the other, it is on the contrary a great law of society that (perhaps for this very reason) a large number of topics are not to be discussed by the sexes in common. It is then a case where nature stimulates and tradition restrains: which shall we declare to be stronger? That depends altogether upon the character of the society in which we live. If it be perfectly free—let us say the society of the Navigator Islands—there the natural attraction of opposite sexes will make their conversation far more agreeable than that of men or women separately.

So it is too among those exceptional sets of people in civilised countries, who brave public opinion so far as to speak their minds to the other sex, and whose conversation is accordingly considered too free by the average of people around them. In this it is natural that the more restrained sex should take the initiative; but if any woman make bold to speak

with perfect freedom among men, and if
she be gifted with the ordinary talents for
conversation, she will be more agreeable
than an intelligent man who says the
same things — or rather she will say
things in a fresher way ; the very situation is somewhat piquant, and so she will
certainly gain by the contrast of sex.   A
small party of men and women of this
sort ought to produce the most amusing
conversation possible.   But I need only
hint how easily such a society may
transgress the due limits, and degenerate
into what the later Athenians thought
brilliant, and collected in a special book·
Nor will freedom, far less audacity, in
conversation redeem ignorance, rudeness,
or graver vices.

Take another kind of society, either
one of Puritanical strictness—I remember
when the word *girl* was thought rather
improper in religious Dublin society, you
should say *young person*—or else that sort

of foreign society which, from suspicion
and fear, prohibits any intimacy between
young men and women, or brands such
intimacy as foreign to good society. There
can be no doubt that here contrast of sex
is fatal to conversation, which will become
constrained, conventional, and occupied
with topics either too trivial or too serious
for proper recreation. Women living under
these conditions find no interest in studying the subjects that interest men—especially politics ; and so it comes to pass that
in the greater part of orderly modern
English society, a company of men only is
thought more agreeable than a mixed one
—even though the ladies be not so strict
as in the extreme cases mentioned, but
merely understand domestic and moral
topics, to the exclusion of public affairs.

§ 49. This being the general aspect of
the problem, it only remains to apply the
principles already attained in the case of
a dialogue with one of the other sex. In

old times, that extreme form of courtesy
called gallantry was thought the proper
way to please a woman. It is now
almost vulgar, and the man who desires to
flatter an intelligent woman, and interest
her, will take care to treat her as an intellectual equal, not as a plaything or a pet.
A man who seizes the opportunity of a
conversation to consult a lady on some
social difficulty, or makes her for the
moment his confidante in some matter not
to be divulged, will be almost sure to find
her agreeable and sympathetic.

Men, especially elderly men, are far
more easily flattered by women, and more
easily carried away by such flattery.
For this reason I think it unnecessary,
nay, perhaps mischievous, to discuss how
ladies use this powerful engine in society.
The real difficulty under which they labour
as to conversation is to hit off the right
mean between prudery and its opposite,
to know how far to speak out frankly,

and when to put a bridle on the talker
who threatens to overstep the bounds of
the reverence due to ourselves and to one
another.

This reverence is, of course, due most
especially to youth, and elderly people
who discuss before young boys and girls
any topics not perfectly pure, are guilty
of such a crime in conversation as can
hardly be censured too severely. Before
other elderly people the case is somewhat
different, and things may then be said
or implied which are not suited for
discussion in the presence of the young.
But above all, let us be strict in checking
this kind of licence, which is so apt to
take possession of the baser minds among
us, and degrade conversation—the recreation of intellect and the mirror of social
goodness—into a serious mischief.

§ 50. What I have said above concerning the advantage of treating the other
sex as strict equals in conversation, is but

another instance of the principle already
laid down (§ 40), that no really bright
social intercourse is possible without
equality. There is, in fact, nothing so
democratic as good conversation, nothing
so Protestant, for we must seem to assert
our private judgment, even where we
assent. And as a man does best to seek
a woman's opinion, and ask her advice,
so as to make her feel on the same plane,
a woman who desires to be agreeable may
differ without hesitation from the opinions
expressed by men, and assert her independ-
ence of judgment, and her consequent
right to take part in a real conversation.
A woman who does this, even ignorantly,
or without good reasons, is better than
she who sits down and acquiesces in
whatever is said by men ; this mental
submission is the acknowledgment of
inferiority which is subversive of all
pleasant talk.

Degrees of Intimacy

§ 51. The only other classification of
the members of a small society worth
making here is in accordance with the
various degrees of their previous intimacy.
They may either be a family party consisting of near relations, or a friendly
party consisting of intimate friends, or
a party of casual acquaintances who meet
not unfrequently, or a chance collection
of almost strangers.   In all these cases
there is naturally some modification in the
conditions of agreeable talking.   And first
of all let us mention to those who think
it is not worth while taking trouble to
talk in their family circle, or who read the
newspaper at meals, that they are making
a mistake which has far-reaching conse-
quences.   It is nearly as bad as those
convent schools or ladies' academies, where
either silence or a foreign tongue is im-

posed at meals, and concerning which I
have already spoken (§ 37). Whatever
people may think of the value of theory,
there is no doubt whatever that practice
is necessary for conversation, and it is at
home, among those who are intimate, and
free in expressing their thoughts, that this
practice must be sought. It is thus, and
thus only, that young people can go out
into the world properly provided with the
really universal introduction to society—
agreeable manners.

Here, then, conversation is not so much
a recreation as a duty, and so becomes
too grave a matter for this book. I will
merely say a word upon the position of
a guest who is introduced into such a
party, to whose daily trifles, family feuds,
or friendships, he is a stranger. It is
of course the first duty of the family
not to monopolise the topics by discussing family histories unknown and uninteresting beyond their circle. Menander

long ago complained of the misfortune of falling into a party of this kind.[1]   On the other hand, the stranger assumes a temporary interest in affairs outside his ordinary life, and merely for the sake of his hosts.   But if he is appealed to as an umpire by members who habitually differ in opinion (and this he will easily note) he will be very wary of giving a decision, and rather discover that there is truth on each side of the question.

§ 52. Far easier is the position of a party of intimate friends.   They have probably become friends simply because they enjoy each other's society, and have many topics of interest in common.   It requires no exertion to make them talk, and they will readily condone moments of taciturnity and depression in one or more members of the party.   They want no advice, and need no instruction, for they possess the only true and permanent

[1] Cf. my *Social Life of Greece*, p. 317.

human bond which keeps men and women ever sympathetic, and ever agreeable to one another.

§ 53. As regards a company of strangers, on the contrary, all the principles stated in the earlier parts of this book will have their clearest application. To interest or to fascinate a stranger requires all the gifts there enumerated, and in proportion as we possess them, and take pains to use them, we shall succeed in turning the stranger into the friend. There is no greater test of conversational powers than to go into a company of strangers, to make them feel at home, to turn their minds to some common thought, and establish an agreeable and sociable spirit where there was at first nothing but coldness and diffidence. To do this single-handed is a feat beyond the power of most people. But if several persons make an effort in the same direction, the combination will effect what a single genius can hardly accomplish.

M

Nothing proves more conclusively the value of practice in these things than the fact that the higher classes, who are compelled through constant moving about both at home and abroad to converse frequently with casual acquaintances, and who in various society often meet strangers—these are the people in whom we generally observe ease of conversation under such conditions. We set it down to good breeding, but this means that not only they but their ancestors have been practising it. Hereditary virtues have not been created with less labour than any other virtues. Generally they require the efforts of several generations, and are from this point of view the most arduous and meritorious of all.

The Topics of Conversation — Serious and Trivial

§ 54. Having now exhausted the subjective side, that is to say the qualities in the speaker and the conditions among the hearers which make or mar conversation, it is natural to proceed to the objective side, and see how far we can classify the topics which form the matter of our talk. Of course a division of the actual subjects under specific heads would require an encyclopædia, and even then would never be complete, for the very essence of good conversation is to wander through all possible things in heaven, in earth, and under the earth, without bond or limit, the only universal condition being that we should range far and near and seek all possible variety, or rather let ourselves drift from point to point, than determine to hold a fixed course. The quantity, therefore, of subjects being infinite, and so not to be described, we must content ourselves with regarding them in quality as either serious or trivial ; in relation to the speakers, as either universal or personal ; in the mode of treatment, as handled either in council, in controversy, or in exposition.

§ 55. Our theory has declared itself long ago against over-seriousness in conversation. This caution is specially necessary nowadays,—when people read so many books and work so hard,—lest they should regard conversation as merely a deliberate method of instruction and channel of improvement. Nay, these very objects will be far better attained indirectly and by the way, while the company is indulging in talk as a recreation.

But it is almost needless to say that the most solid and lasting recreation, the most excellent refreshment of the soul, is to be had from very serious converse, especially where not more than two or three are

gathered together, and to exclude this precious comfort from any theory of conversation would be absurd.   On the other
hand, when two people are earnestly
engaged on a really serious topic, we may
leave them to themselves, and need not
intrude upon them any idle considerations
as to their manner of treating it.   For this
is not conversation in the proper sense.
'In this frame of mind,' says Hawthorne
in his *Transformation* (chap. ii.), 'men
sometimes find their profoundest truths
side by side with the idlest jest, and utter
one or the other, apparently without distinguishing which is the more valuable or
assigning any considerable value to either.'
He hits the truth exactly.   Great seriousness is as detrimental to a general talk
as excessive trifling.   For as the latter fails
after a few moments to interest people who
have any sense, so the former fails to
recreate or amuse, and is in fact earnest
work invading the proper domain of leisure·

There is therefore no general direction
here possible save to avoid both extremes,
or rather to avoid persistence in either
extreme, for it is better to have them
in turn, than to cultivate subjects which
are indifferent. Brilliant talk alternates
between grave and gay, and above all
shuns dryness, detail, minuteness—in a
word, tediousness.

The moment at which, by common consent, people talk trivialities, is the moment
of first introduction. And here the weather
is almost invariably the first pawn to be
moved. It is amazing what triteness and
endless repetition are tolerated by society
on this point. The facts stated are common
property, and agreed to by all, so that the
first object of ordinary people seems to be
to express nothing while they are saying
something. Yet I suppose what is sanc-
tioned by almost universal practice must
have some good reason behind it, and
is perhaps meant to give people time

to observe each other without apparent rudeness. This method of opening the game seems, however, so trite that every agreeable person will endeavour to break through mere formality and make the people about him begin to think as soon as possible. On the other hand it is easy to overdo the attempt, and begin with something so serious that the unprepared audience is frightened and chilled. Thus there can be no greater blunder than to inquire suddenly about the state of a man's soul, a sort of *coup* which many pious people have actually thought a decent introduction to a conversation.

THE TOPICS OF CONVERSATION— GENERAL AND PERSONAL

§ 56. Here we have before us one of the most difficult of problems, and which I shall rather state than attempt to solve.

Should we aim at making our conversation universal in subject, or should we prefer it to be on personal topics, such as gossip or scandal—the character of some mutual friend, an enemy, and so forth ?   There is not the smallest doubt that if we wish it to be profitable and improving, personal topics should be avoided, and that we should talk not about people but about things.   And when an assembly of really cultivated people discusses literary questions, such as the comparative merits of poets or novelists, there is not only great pleasure to be gained from such a society, but the after-taste is good, and men feel that their leisure has not been in vain.

On the other hand, it is idle to deny that in most companies people have not read or thought enough to join in such a conversation or to enjoy it ; whereas details of personal life, the latest anecdote, the facts or surmises about some scandal, the adverse criticism of some acquaintance—

all this kind of thing, ranging from harmless gossip into libellous scandal, is deeply interesting to almost everybody, and though by no means improving is always entertaining.

But even so let the scandalmonger beware. If his ordinary topics are the characters of his acquaintances, he will soon find himself shunned or treated with suspicion by society ; and nothing so completely kills all the pleasure of a company as a protest from any one present that he will not have his absent friend maligned, and that he denies the truth of what has just been said. To apologise to him for the statement or to resist him with argument is equally fatal, for the whole ease and good temper required for pleasant talk has vanished for that occasion.

§ 57. For these reasons, unless the talk consists of confidences between two people who thoroughly understand one another, in which case I hold personal topics to be

far the easiest and the most agreeable, our
theory tells us to raise if possible the
gossip about individuals into reflections
upon classes or even principles.   Thus, if
a young lady remarks that such a man is
conceited, you may raise the question how
far conceit is excusable ; or whether it
may not be commendable ; whether it
means a false estimate of poor endow-
ments or a just estimate of considerable
attainments, and so forth.   Or else you
may inquire whether men or women are
the more conceited as a rule, and whether
Aristotle was not right in setting down
over-bashfulness as a vice.   Beginning
then with the characters of individuals,
which is the easiest prologue, and in
which somebody will always be ready to
start, we disengage the general or common
feature, and not only avoid personalities,
but enable those who have no knowledge
and interest about the person described to
join in the broader discussion of social

ethics.   And let it not be imagined that
because these things have been discussed
millions of times they are therefore trite
and dull.   Just as each succeeding
philosopher insists on thinking out again
for himself what seems to have been
thoroughly exhausted by his predecessors,
so every member of society thinks himself
capable of deciding over again upon questions which have been settled by thousands
of other people to their own satisfaction.

I said above (§ 32) that when two people
only are conversing, personal topics are
most suitable, and of all these the confessions of either to the other are the best.
In the first place nothing is so agreeable to
most men as to have their own history the
object of sympathy, and that is the meaning of the trite adage: Talk to people
about themselves, and not about yourself.
And again, nothing can be more fascinating than genuine autobiography—I mean
confessions of human experience not set

down for the public, not trussed and
cooked for their use, but the real out-
speaking of a human heart.   This it is
which makes autobiographies so popular
as books ; though as soon as any one be-
gins to confess to the public, all the real
depth and intimacy of his experience
vanish, generally to make way for exhibi-
tions of morbid vanity.   It is only one
man in a million who has the modesty
and the shamelessness, the innocence and
the impudence to unveil all his real life to
the world of strangers.[1]

TOPICS OF CONVERSATION—MODES OF TREATMENT

§ 58. Finally, we may distinguish the
mode in which all subjects may be treated,
just as the old rhetoricians divided the

[1] I may cite the autobiographies of Benvenuto Cellini
and of Alfieri in their complete Italian form as the most
real, if not the only real, specimens I know.

various modes of oratory ; for, as we said
at the outset, conversation may be in
theory regarded as informal rhetoric.   The
old division, then, of orations was based on
the form which the company of hearers
and speakers assumed.   Was it a deliberative assembly, which sat in conclave, as it
were, to find out the truth or the right thing
to do upon an open question ?   Then the
proper form of eloquence was the *Deliberative*, that of the Senate-house or Parlia-
ment, suggesting arguments with gravity
and modesty,[1] receiving with deference
and attention the views of others, stimulat-
ing all to give their opinions.   Was it a
judicial court, where the question was a
dispute, and the speakers had their line determined as plaintiffs or defendants ?   Then
the form was the *Controversial*, in which
each side was bound to make the best of

---

[1] I need hardly say that the present Houses of Par-
liament in England and elsewhere, if we except the
House of Lords, will not serve as specimens.

its own case, and the worst of the adversary's; in which each speaker was to bid for the favour of the court, and only limit the violence of his invective by the fear of alienating the judges of the case, and so defeating the object he had in view. Lastly, was the meeting one which merely came together to be impressed or amused by the display of a single speaker, to whom the topic was prescribed, and whose duty it was to excite the emotions and enlist the sympathy of his hearers? Then the proper form was the *Florid*, or *Epideictic*, as they called it, where display was the object, where pomp and ornament were in their proper place.

§ 59. These distinctions are, with reasonable reservations, clearly applicable to conversation. The best kind is when the subject is discussed by the company as if at an informal council, in which each member gives his opinion and contributes something to the common stock; where

each is not only listened to in turn, but
is expected to speak; and where the variety
of views and of the expression of them
constitutes the very charm of the company.
The more people succeed in adopting this
form of discussion, the more successful
their society will be.   The most perfect
host and hostess are those who induce all
their guests to talk, and elicit even from
the silent and the bashful some stray
sprinkling of intelligence, which gives
additional flavour to the spiritual repast.

It may happen, however, that the topic
is taken up by two leading minds in the
company, and discussed as a controversy,
each putting forth his strength to wrestle
with his friendly adversary.   Then it may
be desirable for the rest to take sides,
and encourage the conflict of wit or
argument.   This sort of conversation may
be exceedingly pleasant, provided the dis-
putants keep their temper, and provided
they do not monopolise too great a share

of the time and attention of the rest.
There is hardly a company which will
not tire of the discussion of a single
subject, however important or interesting.
Nevertheless the controversial form is
distinctly an agreeable and often highly
instructive form of conversation, and many
a society of ordinary people attain to the
enjoyment of an excellent evening by
encouraging two leading spirits to show
their powers.

The same good result may be obtained
when the company come together for the
purpose of hearing some remarkable person, who is held out as the attraction of the
party.   It is not conversation, in any real
sense, unless it stimulates others to speak ;
but still we must include in our survey
those cases where the funny man, or the
Arctic traveller, or the superannuated
detective, or the escaped nihilist, under-
takes to tell his experiences, and delight
us with 'real fiction.'   This is truly the

epideictic or *show-off* style, in which the
solitary speaker is supposed to delight and
display himself without a rival, or with
a rival silenced before him.   Indeed, it is
matter of common remark that two or
three such talkers are apt to neutralise
one another and produce no effect.   Each
is supposed to be afraid of the other, or
jealous of the other, and so wanting in
that spontaneity or *abandon* only attained
in a congenial atmosphere.   This is not
my experience of Irish wits, of whom a
wise English friend often remarked to
me : There is no use in asking one Irishman to dinner ; you must ask another to
draw him out.

Epilogue

§ 60. The theory of conversation here
attempted seems to be completely con-
tained in the foregoing paragraphs, so far
as the author has been able to investigate

N

it. No doubt many of his readers will
wonder that a subject so interesting can
be made so dry, and will complain (in spite
of § 5) that he has not given at least a few
specimens of what he approves.   If he is
unable to compose them, why not cull
them from the best novel literature of the
day ?   It is, of course, quite easy to give
such examples, which can be found in
thousands from the comedies of Sheridan
to the stories of Lever—who was himself, like Sheridan, a great master of conversation.   But who ever profited directly
in his own conversation by reading conversations ?   Who could ever transfer to
ordinary intercourse the imaginary dialogues of romance ?   They may be elabor-
ate and studied, like those of Walter
Scott's heroines, and indeed the lovers'
dialogues of almost all novelists ; or they
may be perfectly natural and easy, like
those of Charles Lever just referred to.
But in either case they are stereotyped in

their book, and are useless even as models. One may quote from them an occasional brilliant or foolish remark, as one may from any book, but that is all.

There is always this difficulty about any practice which has never been reduced to rule, that the laws of it, when set forth in order, seem trivial and dull ; nor will the student believe that such valuable and complicated results can be derived from mere truisms. We are quite accustomed to that surprise in the case of logic. The whole system of human reasoning in all its wonderful intricacy is built up from a few general principles, in themselves perfectly and necessarily obvious, just as the prose of Ruskin and the poetry of Browning are expressed in combinations of twenty-six letters. But as in this case the theory of composing words is easy enough, and yet the art a mystery, which only very few can ever attain in perfection,—each,

too, after his own fashion, and stamped
with his own genius,—so the theory of
conversation may be reduced to a small
number of general observations, and yet
the perfect practice of it is a mystery,
which defies analysis—one of the myriad
manifestations of human genius which all
can admire but no one can ever explain.

THE END

Printed by R. & R. CLARK, *Edinburgh.*